Surviving Trainer and Transport Aircraft of the World

Surviving Trainer and Transport Aircraft of the World

A Global Guide to Location and Types

Don Berliner

Pen & Sword
AVIATION

First published in Great Britain in 2013 by
Pen & Sword Aviation
An imprint of
Pen & Sword Books Ltd
47 Church Street
Barnsley
South Yorkshire
S70 2AS

ISBN 978 1 78159 106 2

A CIP catalogue record for this book is
available from the British Library

Typeset in 10.5pt Palatino by Mac Style, Driffield, East Yorkshire
Printed and bound in India by Replika Press Pvt. Ltd.

Pen & Sword Books Ltd incorporates the Imprints of Pen & Sword Aviation, Pen & Sword
Family History, Pen & Sword Maritime, Pen & Sword Military, Pen & Sword Discovery,
Wharncliffe Local History, Wharncliffe True Crime, Wharncliffe Transport, Pen & Sword Select,
Pen & Sword Military Classics, Leo Cooper, The Praetorian Press, Remember When,
Seaforth Publishing and Frontline Publishing

For a complete list of Pen & Sword titles please contact
PEN & SWORD BOOKS LIMITED
47 Church Street, Barnsley, South Yorkshire, S70 2AS, England
E-mail: enquiries@pen-and-sword.co.uk
Website: www.pen-and-sword.co.uk

Contents

Introduction

While fighters were the main aerial defensive weapons of the war, and bombers the main aerial offensive weapons, if it hadn't been for the often little-known other types of aircraft, it would have been impossible for the fighters and bombers to do their much more public and glamorous jobs.

Without tens of thousands of trainers, the heroic pilots would have been just another group of surface-bound soldiers and seamen. Without thousands of transports, fuel and food and weapons and men would have languished far behind the lines with no way to become useful.

Without reconnaissance airplanes, there would not have been enough known about the enemy to decide which targets were most vital, and then, after they had been selected and bombed, to determine if another mission was required.

Other types simply had little or no precedents in the military air services. Gliders – small ones for training and much larger ones designed to carry soldiers and/or cargo – were a World War II phenomenon. The same can be said for rotary-wing aircraft, mainly helicopters. While the first crude attempts to fly them date back to pre-World War I days, none went into quantity production until the early 1940s.

For many years military aircraft had been used for experimental purposes, such as flying with alternative engines, and being armed with ever-larger guns, but the idea of aircraft meant solely for experimentation was something new.

All phases of aviation were expanding, and that of military aviation was no exception.

Chapter 1

Transports

Introduction

Highly specialized types of airplanes such as bombers and fighters require years to design and prove before they are ready for production, let alone action. Transports, on the other hand, could usually be purchased "off the shelf" from manufacturers who had been building them for very similar civilian purposes. As an example, the Douglas C-47 was little more than a well-proven DC-3 airliner with uncomfortable seats, a less attractive paint job and some grumpy crew chief in place of a pretty young stewardess. Since the passengers didn't have to pay for their tickets, the passengers' complaints were ignored, and the airplanes, which had been snatched from their civilian jobs like those they were to carry, fulfilled a need that would otherwise have required a long and expensive period of gestation.

United States of America

Lockheed C-36 Electra (civil 10A)

The 1930s was a time for airlines and those who designed and built their airplanes to take a major step into the future. Fabric covering, open cockpits and fixed landing gears might have been acceptable in the 1920s. But if airlines were ever to grow and actually return a profit without government subsidies that could be revoked at any moment, big changes were required.

It wouldn't be easy and it wouldn't be quick. Metal covering for fuselages and wings and tails would involve new, lightweight materials and new fabrication techniques. It would be necessary to develop practical retractable landing gears that were not merely take-off gears that threatened to collapse on the next hard landing. And pilots would have to be convinced that they could fly well even if the wind wasn't blowing in their faces. An entire culture had to change, and this would involve some very large risks. Military air arms were faced with the same problems, but lacked the available money needed to pay for the extensive research and development. They would have to rely on those who built civil airplanes to lead the way.

Among the first to charge into this little-known territory was the struggling little Lockheed Aircraft Corp., which was just starting to attract some much needed attention with its single-engined, high-wing Vega, a small airliner that offered speed equal to anything the U.S. Army or U.S. Navy could field. But it was built of wood, a symbol of the past.

In February 1934, a few months before the first flight of deHavilland's futuristic Comet Racer, which would be flown to victory in the London to Melbourne MacRobertson Race, Lockheed flew its prototype Model 10 Electra. This was the company's first twin-engined design and was aimed directly at the growing airline industry. With a pair of new 450hp Pratt & Whitney Wasp Jr radial engines, it was meant to cruise at 190mph with 10 passengers.

As with any major departure from traditional airplane design, this one had its problems, many of which were solved by a talented graduate student assistant, Clarence "Kelly' Johnson, who went on to direct Lockheed's history-making "Skunk Works" advanced design center. The Model 10 Electra was a success, at least partly because the U.S. Government had banned passenger flights by single-engined airplanes for safety reasons.

Almost 150 examples of the Models A to E were built for civilian use, but by the late 1930s newer and larger airliners such as the Douglas DC-3 were coming into use. In 1936, a single XC-35 was modified for the U.S. Army Air Corps from a standard Model 10 for highly successful experiments with the first pressurized cabin.

The most famous of the 10s was the modified10E in which Amelia Earhart and navigator Fred Noonan almost pulled off a round-the-world flight in 1937 before disappearing somewhere in the Pacific Ocean and becoming a permanent object of search efforts.

The Army bought 13 as UC-36s and a single Y1C-37, and impressed 15 more from private owners, while the Navy bought three as R2O-1. They did yeoman work on a wide variety of military support missions, while a few found themselves in the Spanish Civil War. Perhaps the biggest contribution of the Model 10 was to lead to a whole series of Lockheed twin-engined airliners including the Super Electra and the Lodestar and then to the Hudson and Ventura bombers.

Specifications

Length: 38ft 7in
Wingspan: 55ft 0in
Height: 10ft 1in
Wing area: 458 sq ft

Empty weight: 6,655lb
Maximum speed: 200mph
Maximum range: 715 miles
Service ceiling: 19,400ft
Rate of climb: 1,000ft/min

Surviving Examples

XC-35
USAAC 36-353 – U.S. National Air & Space Museum

C-36
USAAF 42-56638 – Pima Air and Space Museum
CF-TCA, c/n 1112 – Canadian Aviation Museum

XR2O-1
BuAer 0267 – New England Air Museum

Douglas C-39/R2D (DC-2)

The unforgettable DC-3 started out, reasonably enough, as the Douglas DC-1. Propelled by the same winds of change that blew Lockheed's Electra into being, the sole DC-1 flew a year earlier and quickly led to the more practical DC-2, which carried 14 passengers at almost the same speed as the Electra, and offered unprecedented efficiency and reliability. Not long after the prototype Electra took to the air, a production DC-2 of Royal Dutch Airlines placed second, to a purpose-built racer, in the London to Melbourne Race, signaling a new age in commercial transportation.

Although fewer than 60 DC-2s served with the U.S. Army, variations carried seven different designations: C-32, C-33, C-34,

Now, with an airplane that could take off and climb on one engine, there was a margin of safety that could be promoted to everyone's benefit. The DC-1, however, was all but forgotten as DC-2s began to roll off the assembly line and appear at every airport served by Trans-Continental and Western Airlines (TWA).

The DC-2 changed the thinking of everyone connected with what was becoming the airline industry, with comfort joining safety and ease of maintenance in their vocabulary. It was only natural that the military would see it as a ready-made troop and later cargo carrier, after a few fairly simple modifications.

A single 16-passenger XC-32 was ordered by the Army Air Corps in 1936, and later became a flying command post. The C-32A was a commercial DC-2, 24 of which were impressed by the Army Air Forces in early 1942. Eighteen C-33s were built as cargo planes, having a larger vertical tail, sturdier cabin floor and a large cargo door.

The two C-34s were ex-airline airplanes with what was becoming standard interior changes. The first C-33 became the prototype of the C-39, with a DC-3 tail and more powerful engines.

The sole C-41 was a C-39 having 1,200hp Wright R-1820 engines, built expressly for Air Force chief General Henry "Hap" Arnold. The sole C-41 was similar. Yet another VIP transport – the C-42 – was joined by a pair of converted C-39s.

With the approach of the C-47/DC-3, everything else became relegated to minor duties.

C-38, C-39, C-41 and C-42. More C-39s were acquired (by confiscation from airlines) by the USAAC than any other version. Even though it was actually a composite of the DC-2 and DC-3, that version will be used here as the standard.

The DC-1 flew for the first time in July 1933 and served as the prototype of the DC-2. It carried 12 passengers and was powered by a pair of 690hp Wright R-1020 radial engines with variable-pitch three-bladed propellers that gave it a cruising speed of over 180mph. It was in competition with Boeing's monoplane Model 247, and both were the immediate result of the government's banning of airliners with major structural members made from wood. A fatal accident with a wooden Fokker Trimotor had produced an uproar which quickly led to all-metal airliners.

Marginal performance had long been accepted for airliners, along with the need for a spirit of adventure on the part of passengers.

Specifications

Length: 62ft 6in
Wingspan: 83ft 0in
Height: 15ft 10in

Wing area: 940 sq ft
Empty weight: 12,455lb
Maximum speed: 210mph
Combat radius: 1,085 miles
Service ceiling: 22,750ft
Rate of climb: 1,030ft/min

Surviving Examples

C-39
USAAC 38-515 – National Museum of the U.S. Air Force

DC-2
NC-1934D – Museum of Flight, Seattle, Washington

Lockheed C-40 (Model 12A Electra Jr)

As might be expected of an airplane named "Junior", it was a smaller version of an original, the Model 10 Electra, but using the same Pratt & Whitney 450hp Wasp Jr engines and thus being faster. Aimed at feeder airlines, it appealed to few of them, as the trend was increasingly toward greater passenger capacity, seen as the most direct route to airline profitability. More than a few went to large industrial corporations for use as some of the first executive airplanes, while others were bought by the U.S. Government to be used as military staff transports as the Army's C-40 and the Navy's JO-1 and JO-2.

Foreign sales were brisk and varied. Two went to British Airways and were flown over Germany and Italy before the war by Sidney Cotton's secret reconnaissance group, fitted with hidden cameras. Three dozen were sold to the Royal Netherlands East Indies Army

Air Force, with almost half of them equipped with machine guns and bomb racks for use as trainers.

One model 12A, stripped down and filled with extra fuel tanks, was flown by Milo Burcham on the 2,043-mile 1937 Bendix Trophy Race course from Burbank, California, to Cleveland, Ohio, non-stop at 184mph. Others were used for research into hot-air de-icing and the practicality of operating twin-engined airplanes with tricycle landing gear from aircraft carriers.

Almost half the Electra Jrs flown by the USAAC had been privately owned airplanes taken over after the war began. A total of 130 of all models and designations were built before Lockheed became so busy manufacturing P-38 Lightning fighters and Hudson bombers that it was forced to shut down the production line.

Specifications

Length: 36ft 4in
Wingspan: 49ft 6in
Height: 9ft 9in
Wing area: 352 sq ft
Empty weight: 5,765lb
Maximum speed: 225mph
Maximum range: 800 miles
Service ceiling: 22,900ft
Rate of climb: 1,140ft/min

Surviving Examples

USAAC 38-540 – Yanks Air Museum, Chino Airport, California
c/n 1219 – Canadian Aviation Museum as CF-CCT

Beech C-43 Traveler (Model 17 Staggerwing)

When economic times turn bad, one of the most obvious ways for a large company to cut back on expenses is by getting rid of its fast, comfortable executive transport, or by not buying one in the first place. It therefore took great courage to launch a completely new and even more expensive airplane for company use in the middle of the Great Depression of the 1930s.

That was exactly what Beech did when it revealed, in late 1932, its Model 17 to the public as the fastest, best equipped and most comfortable way to carry company big-wigs on more-or-less vital trips. Surprisingly, enough people found the money to purchase 18 of the costly airplanes in the first year, and more than 400 by late 1941.

Nicknamed "Staggerwing" by its friends due to the reverse-stagger of its wings, it combined traditional wood-and-fabric structure with some of the latest ideas in aerodynamics, such as retractable landing gear (after the fixed-gear prototype), a low-drag windshield and excellent fairings into a package that would top 200mph on the 450 horsepower of a Pratt & Whitney R-985 Wasp Jr.

Competition again brought a commercial airplane to the attention of the public and the military. The 1936 Bendix Trophy victory by two women who out-raced and out-lasted a field of "unlimited" manufactured and custom-built airplanes was a public demonstration of both speed and reliability. Enough Staggerwings were sold to keep the small company in business.

As World War II approached, small air forces bought small numbers of Model 17s and quickly found new uses for them. In the Spanish Civil War, several were rigged out as bombers. In the Sino-Japanese War, the Chinese used them as ambulance planes. The Finns had one in use for liaison work.

It was only when the USAAF ordered 270 Model 17s and then impressed 118 from private owners that the airplane became a major military type, with those going to the U.S. Navy becoming GB-1 and -2. An additional 106 went to the Royal Air Force and Navy to bring the total in uniform to more than 500.

Throughout its production run, the Staggerwing remained virtually unchanged, which made re-conversion to civilian use after the war a fairly simple procedure. A few more were built after the war, but the emergence of the sleek V-tailed Bonanza was too much for the venerable biplane to overcome. The new airplane was considerably smaller, more economical and had equal performance. While the price of a new one has increased 100 times, it has retained its modern look for over half a century. The Staggerwing, one of the most modern-looking of biplanes, has become one of the most treasured of vintage designs.

Specifications

Length: 26ft 10in
Wingspan: 32ft 0in
Height: 8ft 0in
Wing area: 297 sq ft
Empty weight: 2,540lb
Maximum speed: 212mph
Maximum range: 580 miles
Service ceiling: 25,000ft
Rate of climb: 1,500ft/min

Surviving Museum Examples

UC-43
USAAF 44-76068 – National Museum of the U.S. Air Force
NC-15840 – U.S. National Air & Space Museum

GB-2
BuAer 23688 – U.S. National Museum of Naval Aviation

Beech C-45/JRB Kansan (Model 18 "Twin Beech")

The ubiquitous "Twin Beech", which first flew in early 1937, appeared in two basic forms: as a utility transport (C-45 Expeditor for the USAAF and JRB for the U.S. Navy) and an advanced trainer (AT-7 Navigator and AT-11 Kansan for the USAAF, and SNB Kansan for the Navy). The basic airframe and the pair of 450hp

Pratt & Whitney R-985 radial engines remained the same, with only necessary changes being made to interior systems.

At the time the U.S.A. entered the war in late 1941, fewer than 50 Beech 18s had been sold, while the visually similar, but slightly larger, Lockheed Electra had gone into service by the hundreds, thanks to its greater speed and capacity. When Lockheed became swamped with orders for its P-38 fighters and Hudson patrol bombers, military orders for the Electra were switched to Beechcraft. The Model 18 was suddenly in great demand.

With fewer than 500 airplanes built by Beechcraft since its founding, the impact of the war was enormous, as more than 5,700 military airplanes based on the Model 18 rolled off the assembly lines in a few years. Of them, almost 1,800 were passenger/cargo planes (1,400 for the USAAF and 375 for the Navy), while more than 3,900 were trainers (2,700 for the USAAF and 1,200 for the Navy. In addition, some 60 were F-2 photo-reconnaissance versions.

In 1943, all small "C" (Cargo) types were re-designated "UC" for Utility Cargo, though little changed otherwise. They were used to transport people (mainly "high-value" types such as senior officers) as well as small amounts of cargo which would not justify the much larger and expensive-to-operate C-46s and C-47s.

Most World War II types began to fade away when the war ended, but military versions of the Beech 18 soldiered on. An estimated 900 UC-45s were re-manufactured by Beech for the USAAF and others for the Navy to conform with the latest civilian model, the D18S. They had re-built fuselages and wing center sections, as well as strengthened landing gear.

The lifetime of the series of small twins was impressive, with the USAF flying them until 1963, the Navy until 1972 and the U.S. Army as late as 1976. By then, a string of small firms had developed major modifications to extend the useful life of the 18 with stretched fuselages, tricycle landing gears and ultimately turboprop engines. Some can still be seen in the air, carrying loads ranging from small packages to sky-divers.

Specifications

Length: 34ft 2in
Wingspan: 47ft 8in
Height: 9ft 8in
Wing area: 349 sq ft
Empty weight: 6,175lb
Maximum speed: 225mph
Maximum range: 1,200 miles
Service ceiling: 26,000ft
Rate of climb: 1,850ft/min

Surviving Examples

UC-45
Planes of Fame

C-45H
USAAF – National Museum of the U.S. Air Force

C-45J
BuAer 44588 – March Field Air Museum

UC-45J Expeditor
BuAer 29646 & 39213 – Pima Air and Space Museum

JRB-1
U.S. Naval Aviation Museum

JRB-4
BuAer 44676 – Musee de l'Air, Paris
BuAer 90536 – U.S. Marine Corps Aviation Museum, Quantico, Virginia

Curtiss C-46/R5C Commando

The two most successful twin-engined transport airplanes of the war were both American: the Curtiss C-46 and the Douglas C-47, both of which started out as civilian airliners. While the C-47 was an instant world-wide success carrying paying customers, the C-46 got a later start and aroused limited interest among the airlines before both types were drafted into the Army.

The C-46 bore no resemblance to any Curtiss predecessor, coming along immediately after the two-winged, fabric-covered Condor. The Commando, on the other hand, was the most technologically advanced transport of its day, designed for a pressurized fuselage which would have enabled it to fly higher and thus faster than any of its rivals. Though it was never so equipped, almost all production models were powered by a pair of the latest 2,100hp Pratt & Whitney R-2800 engines.

The prototype, with 1,600hp Wright engines and twin vertical tails, flew for the first time in March 1940. The USAAF was not interested in this version, which was eventually sold to the British Overseas Airways Corporation. Six months after the first flight, 46 much-modified CW-20Bs with single large tails were bought by the USAAF as C-46As. Soon, 200 were on order, as the military began to take the airplane seriously as it struggled to re-equip with vast numbers of modern aircraft.

The orders for C-46As grew to almost 1,500, with most having double freight-loading doors, strengthened floors and a power-operated winch help move large items more quickly. For troop carrier missions, 40 folding seats were available, though the Commando was used less for this purpose than was the C-47.

The C-46 established its reputation as a cargo hauler on flights over the Himalayas between India and China – a route known as "The Hump" – with dangerously heavy loads and using the most primitive airstrips at both ends of the flight. Usually flying without fighter escort and suffering predictable losses, the freight service was considered worth the hazards.

After the war, the lack of interest in the Commando on the part of major airlines continued, but many were sold as surplus to recently-established carriers, thanks to their low initial cost. Unfortunately, the ability to cram vast loads into the cavernous

interior led to several highly publicized crashes, some of aircraft carrying as many as 90 to 100 desperate refugees who had no affordable alternative.

Specifications

Length: 76ft 4in
Wingspan: 108ft 1in
Height: 21ft 9in
Wing area: 1,360 sq ft
Empty weight: 29,300lb
Maximum speed: 235mph
Maximum range: 2,950 miles.
Service ceiling: 27,600ft
Rate of climb: 1,300ft/min

Surviving Examples

C-46A
USAAF 42-101115 – Miho Air Base, Japan
USAAF 43-7084 – Brazil Air Force Museum, Campo dos Alphonsos
USAAF 43-47218 – Yanks Air Museum, Chino, California
USAAF 43-47350 – U.S. National Museum of Naval Aviation (as R5C)

C-46D
USAAF 44-77559 – Planes of Fame
USAAF 44-77575 – Castle AFB Museum, California
USAAF 44-77592 – War Memorial, Seoul, South Korea
USAAF 44-77635 – Pima Air and Space Museum
USAAF 44-78015 – National Museum of the U.S. Air Force

C-46F

USAAF 44-78663 – Commemorative Air Force (CAF), Midland, Texas

USAAF 44-78772 – National Air & Space Museum, at Glenn Curtiss Museum

USAAF 44-78774 – Southern California Wing of CAF

R5C-1

BuAer 39611 – U.S. National Museum of Naval Aviation

Douglas C-47/R4D Skytrain/Dakota

It served the military in the air much like the Jeep did on the ground, being able to go anywhere on any mission by flying out of anything that could briefly pass as an airfield. With the knowledge gained from hundreds of DC-3s operated by airlines all over the world, the C-47 had few bad habits and could be maintained under the crudest of conditions. In a word, it was a "classic".

It was born as the DC-1, a prototype airliner that first flew in 1933 and made everything else obsolete. Quickly enlarged into the 14-seat DC-2, of which almost 200 were built, it taught the airlines a new way of doing things. The DC-2, in turn, soon gave way to the DC-3, the first "wide-body", which had an additional seat in each row and could carry 50 per cent more passengers at little increase in operating costs.

By the time the U.S.A. entered World War II, an estimated 85 per cent of the world's airlines were using DC-3s to make more profit than they had ever imagined, and were thus able to expand rather than merely survive. Average people – businessmen and tourists – were finally able to afford tickets, and the world quickly began thinking seriously about air travel as a practical alternative to bus,

train or private car. The future, for the airlines, had never looked so bright.

And then came the war, and absolutely everything changed. The aircraft manufacturing industry, which had been struggling to stay alive through the Great Depression, suddenly saw contracts for thousands of fighters and bombers and transports, for which huge factories had to be built and tens of thousands of new employees taught to operate types of machinery whose names many of them had never heard. There was no time to do things carefully and methodically, as the German blitzkrieg tore up huge chunks of once peaceful Europe and the Japanese Empire spread like a brush fire around the Pacific.

The Douglas DC-3s that had introduced thousands of men and women to leisure flying, became commonplace in all theaters of war as they hauled men and freight into barely sufficient airstrips in the jungle and anywhere else where a flat patch of land could be found. Once in the air, they reverted to airliners, although airliners that had to face anti-aircraft fire and fighters without defensive armament.

C-47s opened the route to China over the Himalayas in fierce weather, supplying the Chinese who had been fighting Japan; the route was later taken over by C-46s that could fly higher with heavier loads. When it came to the Allied invasion of occupied Europe, it was C-47s that towed hundreds of gliders and delivered thousands of paratroops. Later, they supplied resistance forces with food and guns and ammunition and hope.

Even after World War II, the C-47 refused to be discarded. Hundreds were sold as surplus to returning airmen who fancied themselves the proprietors of small airlines or freight lines, but who soon learned there was more to running an airline than knowing how to fly. A few, like Flying Tiger Airlines, survived. When the Viet Nam war broke out, the C-47 became a combat airplane, armed with modern Gatling guns that poured thousands of rounds into hidden jungle outposts.

In all the years of its military operations, what is popularly known as the C-47 flew under numerous official designations (C-47, C-48, C-49, C-50, C-51, C-52 and C-53; the U.S. Navy's R4D; the U.S.S.R.'s Li-2), and names both official and unofficial (Skytrain, Skytrooper, Dakota, Gooney Bird and Gunship). Any airliner of which more than 13,000 were built probably deserves a variety of names and numbers.

Specifications

Length: 63ft 9in
Wingspan: 95ft 6in
Height: 17ft 0in
Wing area: 987 sq ft
Empty weight: 17,000lb
Maximum speed: 224mph
Maximum range: 1,600 miles
Service ceiling: 26,400ft
Rate of climb: 10,000ft in 9:30

Surviving Examples

C-47A

USAAF 42-92647 – Musee de l'Air
USAAF 43-15509 – Imperial War Museum, Duxford

VC-47A

USAAF 43-15579 – March Field Air Museum

C-47B
Canadian National Air Museum

C-47D
USAAF 43-49507 – National Museum of the U.S. Air Force

Mk.IV Dakota
RAF KN645 – RAF Museum, Cosford

R4D-5L
U.S. Museum of Naval Aviation

R4D-8
Pima Air & Space Museum

Douglas C-54/R5D Skymaster

The "big brother" of the C-47, it was the most important four-engined, long-range transport of World War II. The prototype, later designated DC-4E, first flew in June 1938 at the hands of famed racing designer/pilot Ben O. Howard. After tests by United Airlines, the triple-tailed, one-of-a-kind airplane was determined to be too large and too complicated for regular airline use, and was sold to Japan.

A smaller, simpler version was flown in February 1942, but as all production for commercial airlines had been ended for the duration of the war, it became the first of more than 1,000 C-54s for the USAAF. By the time the U.S. military finished using the C-54, well over 60 versions had been created.

The first two dozen were modified from DC-4s originally intended for airline use. What followed was the C-54A, with a beefed-up structure, greater range and an interior suitable for carrying passengers and/or cargo. Some of them were specially outfitted for use in the evacuation of wounded men, while others became R5Ds for the U.S. Navy.

Next came the C-54B, 220 of which were built, including one with a very special interior for British Prime Minister Winston Churchill. The sole VC-54C was for U.S. President Franklin D. Roosevelt and was equipped with a power-driven hoist for the wheelchair required by his increasing debilitation due to polio. At the time, the hoist was kept secret in an effort to maintain FDR's appearance of strength during a period of great wartime-induced national stress.

The C-54D was the major production version, with 380 built with more powerful Pratt & Whitney R-2000 Twin Wasp radial engines. The final World War II version was the C-54E, built to be quickly converted from carrying passengers to carrying freight. One hundred and twenty- five were built, of which 50 became Navy R5D's.

Once the war was over, hundreds of C-54s were reconditioned for airline use, their availability greatly reducing the demand for new aircraft. As a result, Douglas built fewer than 100 new ones before moving on to the larger and faster DC-6. Meanwhile, the USAAF and Navy continued to operate C-54s and R5Ds in large numbers as their primary transport. They served USAF units as late as 1972, and the U.S. Navy until 1974.

Specifications

Length: 93ft 10in
Wingspan: 117ft 6in
Height: 27ft 6in
Wing area: 1,460 sq ft
Empty weight: 38,930lb
Maximum speed: 275mph
Maximum range: 4,000 miles
Service ceiling: 22,300ft

Surviving Examples

VC-54C
USAAF 42-107451 "Sacred Cow" – National Museum of the U.S. Air Force

C-54D
USAAF 42-72261 – Museo del Aire, Quatros Vientos, Spain
USAAF 42-72488 – Pima Air & Space Museum

USAAF 42-72560 – Historic Air Museum, Travis AFB
USAAF 42-72636 – Air Museum, March Field, California

C-54M
USAAF 44-9030 – Dover AFB, Delaware

R5D
BuAer 56514 – March Field Air Museum

Lockheed C-56/C-57/C-59/C-60/C-66/R5O Lodestar

The Lockheed 14 Super Electra had some design problems which resulted in several crashes and the return of most of the others that had been flying for Northwest Airlines. They were rebuilt at the factory with a fuselage extension of 5.5 feet. While this produced a more economical airplane with two more rows of seats, it revealed some control problems. Once the problems were solved, one of

these aircraft became the prototype of the Model 18 Lodestar, which first flew in September 1939.

By this time, however, the Douglas DC-3 was well on its way to becoming the airplane of choice for most U.S. airlines, and so sales of the Model 18 were mainly to foreign airlines, with a total of more than 70 going to, among others, Netherlands East Indies, South African Airways, Trans-Canada Air Lines and BOAC.

What saved the Model 18 was the U.S. military's sudden need for large numbers of transport airplanes as the certainty of a major war became more obvious. With Lockheed having a ready-made assembly line and little demand for its civilian products, the way was clear for the USAAF and the U.S. Navy to order hundreds of Lodestars.

The C-56 series consisted of 35 Lodestars taken back from U.S. airlines and numbered C-56A though C-56E, with the differences being mainly in their engines, most of them using two 1,200hp Wright G-1820 Cyclones. There were 11 numbered in the C-57 range, seven newly built and the rest converted from other versions.

The C-60 was the main version, with 36 C-60s being Model 18-56 with uprated Wright engines, and 325 C-60As being setup for dropping paratroops and using Pratt & Whitney R-1830 Twin Wasp engines. A single C-66 was built with an 11-passenger interior and supplied to the Brazilian Air Force. The designation C-102 was a proposed 21-seat carrier of airborne troops, which was changed to C-60C then finally canceled.

The U.S. Navy received 80 airplanes in the R5O-1 through R5O-6 series, with 38 being R5O-5, which were C-60s set up to carry 14 passengers, and 35 R5O-6 being C-60s for the U.S. Marine Corps.

Of those sold to foreign airlines before the war, 29 were purchased by South African Airways, but the order was transferred to the South African Air Force when war broke out before they could

be delivered. Twelve went to Trans-Canada Air Lines, and nine to BOAC.

After the war, many were converted into executive airplanes with comfortable seats and other non-military fittings.

Specifications

Length: 49ft 10in
Wingspan: 65ft 6in
Height: 11ft 10in
Wing area: 551 sq ft
Empty weight: 12,000lb
Maximum speed: 265mph
Maximum range: 1,700 miles
Service ceiling: 25,400ft
Rate of climb: 1,600ft/min

Surviving Examples

C-56D
South African Airways Museum, Rand, Republic of South Africa

C-60
Norway

C-60A
USAAF 42-55918 – Warner-Robins AFB, Georgia
c/n 2302, N31G – 1940s Air Terminal Museum, Houston, Texas

R5O-5
BuAer 12473 – March Field Air Museum, California

Fairchild C-61/J2K Forwarder

Universally known as the Fairchild 24, it was one of the few private airplanes to survive the Great Depression of the 1930s. When what seemed like equally deserving designs fell by the wayside, hundreds of Fairchild's high-wing tourer sold to private owners at prices ranging from $3,850 in 1933 to almost twice that in 1940 in an era when an average family sedan cost under $1,000.

Unusually for a production line airplane, it was available for almost all its lifetime with a choice of engines: at first either an inline American Cirrus or Menasco, or a Warner radial, ranging from 90 to 125hp. Later, the alternatives were a 145-to-165hp Warner Super Scarab radial or a 145-to-175hp inline Fairchild Ranger.

By the time war broke out and overwhelmed the Depression with widespread industrial expansion, Fairchild had already sold more than 630 '24s, which far exceeded anything else in its class. In the next three years, more than twice as many of the military version would be built, with many of them subsequently converted back into civil airplanes. Fairchild sold its '24 to Temco after the war, but it was difficult to sell shiny new ones when ex-military UC-61s were available at low government surplus prices. As a result, only 280 were built before the line was shut down permanently in 1946.

Of the 1,310 C-61s built, no fewer than 830 (mainly the Warner radial-engined Model 24W) went to Great Britain as part of the Lend-Lease program, many of them for use by the RAF's Air Transport Auxiliary in transporting ferry pilots. Of the rest, they went to the U.S. Army and Navy as light transports, to the U.S. Coast Guard for a variety of purposes and even to the quasi-military Civil Air Patrol for coastal patrol. Some of these actually carried a pair of small bombs which were sometimes used with good effect on unsuspecting German U-Boats.

Those impressed by the USAAF from private owners were 14 given designations UC-61B to J, and nine designated UC-86. Thirteen were impressed by the U.S. Navy as GK-1s, while four were built for the U.S. Coast Guard as J2K-1 and -2. The Royal Air Force received 118 UC-61 as their Argus I, 407 as Argus II, and 306 UC-61K as Argus III. Others went to Australian, Canadian, Finnish, Israeli and Thai air forces.

Specifications

Length: 23ft 10in
Wingspan: 36ft 4in
Height: 7ft 8in
Wing area: 193 sq ft
Empty weight: 1,815lb
Maximum speed: 125mph

Maximum range: 465 miles
Service ceiling: 12,700ft

Surviving Examples

UC-64A
USAAF 44-70296 (as UC-61J) – National Museum of the U.S. Air
  Force (civil F-24C)

Argus
Civil G-AIZE – Royal Air Force Museum, Cosford

Dozens of others were returned to civilian standard and flown as
popular classics.

Norduyn UC-64 Norseman

Rugged – reliable – repairable. These were the goals of the small
Canadian company that built its prototype Norseman in 1935, and
they became the characteristics by which it was known around the
world. A true "bush plane", it was homely and hefty and slow,
in a category which does not concern itself with aeronautical
beauty and speed. It was used for the myriad little jobs spurned by
glamour airplanes and glamour-seeking pilots.

The prototype Norseman was test flown in November 1935 and
soon became the first domestically designed and produced airplane
in Canada. Appropriate to its intended use in the backwoods
where landing strips are scarce, it used floats rather than wheels,
though wheels or skis could replace them with minimal effort.
The prototype (CF-AYO) was sold to Dominion Skyways just two
months later, and went into service.

Realistic tests proved its worth as a tough, easy-to-operate
airplane with reasonable performance from its 325hp Wright
Whirlwind engine. To improve its ability to fly out of short fields
and winding rivers, the second and subsequent versions used a
450hp Pratt & Whitney Wasp. Small numbers of Norsemen were
delivered to small Canadian air services which used them as
flying pack animals, since so much of northern Canada lacked any
meaningful road system.

Sales totaled fewer than 20 by the time the British Commonwealth
entered the war, when the Norseman's hazy future suddenly
became clear. The Royal Canadian Air Force saw its usefulness and
bought 28 of the Mk.IV to use in training radiomen and navigators
under the Commonwealth Air Training Plan. The USAAF soon saw
the Norseman's advantages over American-built utility airplanes,
acquiring seven as YC-64 and then almost 750 more as the C-64A.
The main difference in the C-64A was its increased fuel capacity,

the weight of which was off-set by the use of a more powerful version of the Wasp engine.

A primary use of the Norseman by the USAAF was in Alaska, which resembles northern Canada's terrain, minimal population density and lack of roads. Others were operated in Europe and elsewhere, including six C-64B on floats by the U.S. Army Corps of Engineers. Three C-64B served with the U.S. Navy as floatplanes.

Orders continued, with additional Mk.IVs for the RCAF. When the USAAF began making plans to buy up to 600 more C-64As that would be built under license by Aeronca, the plan failed to progress.

After the war, production rights were acquired by Canadian Car & Foundry for the Mk.V which had metal wings and more power. This scheme ended when the prototype was lost in a fire in 1951.

Norduyn struggled on, providing support for quite a few airplanes that were still serving civilian and military operators, and even built three Mk.Vs before the story came to an end in 1959. An airplane that had an excellent combination of performance and cost could no longer compete with newer designs.

Specifications (UC-64A)

Length: 31ft 9in
Wingspan: 51ft 6in
Height: 10ft 1in
Wing area: 325 sq ft
Loaded weight: 7,400lb
Maximum speed: 162mph
Maximum range: 1,150 miles
Service ceiling: 17,000ft
Rate of climb: 590ft/min

Surviving Examples

Norseman I
CF-AYO (prototype) – Canadian Aviation & Space Museum

YC-64
USAAF 42- – U.S. National Air & Space Museum

UC-64A
USAAF 44-70296 – National Museum of the U.S. Air Force
USAAF 44-70546 – Norwegian Aviation Museum, Bodoe, Norway
  (as LN-PAB)

Norseman VI
RCAF 787 – Canadian Air & Space Museum, Ottawa

Norseman Mk.
British Columbia Aviation Museum

Lockheed C-69 Constellation

For any manufacturer known for its solid, practical twin-engined transports, moving ahead to a pressurized four-engined airliner was a big step. It would eventually be followed by even larger steps into the advanced-technology future with the Mach 4 SR-71 Blackbird and the F-117, the world's first production stealth combat airplane. A priceless reputation was being created.

The origins of the "Connie" can be traced back to 1937 when, at the urging of Howard Hughes, Lockheed began designing a novel four-engined, pressurized airliner to carry 40 passengers from coast to coast, non-stop. This Model L-044 Excalibur may

The first prototype of the Constellation flew in January 1943, powered by troublesome 2,200hp Wright R-3350 Cyclone II engines. By the time the war ended, only 19 had been built, and not all of those were C-69s. The first deliveries to airlines began just two months after the war's end, with the first regularly-scheduled trans-Atlantic service beginning four months after that. Less than a year and a half later, Pan American started the first regular around-the-world service.

While the C-69 Constellation had minimal impact on World War II, later versions such as the C-121 developed from the Super Constellation, served in a variety of roles. One served as President Dwight Eisenhower's airplane, another carried Gen. Douglas McArthur, and several carried elaborate electronic gear and flew classified payloads on mysterious Cold War missions.

have been a preliminary design "cover story" for the subsequent L-049, the handiwork of such future Lockheed legends as Kelly Johnson and Hal Hibbard. As the Constellation, it would introduce a variety of new ideas that would become industry standards.

The airframe, alone, had more than the usual number of unconventional lines. The gracefully tapered wing, spanning 126 feet, was a scaled-up version of the one then flying on P-38 Lightning fighters. The fuselage was slim and fully tapered, while the set of three small vertical tails was chosen to keep the overall height low enough to fit into existing large hangars.

Inside, it had a thermal de-icing system that kept the leading edges of the wings and tail free of ice, the build-up of which had long posed serious problems. The controls were hydraulically boosted, as fully manual controls were considered too heavy on such a large airplane. No sooner had the airliner design been finalized than it was being considered as a long-range bomber, the XB-30, though this idea never got very far, and one suspects that the design might have ended up so extensively modified that its origin would have been lost.

Specifications

Length: 116ft 2in
Wingspan: 126ft 2in
Height: 24ft 9in
Wing area: 1,654 sq ft
Empty weight: 79,700lb
Maximum speed: 377mph
Maximum range: 5,400 miles
Service ceiling: 24,000ft
Rate of climb: 1,620ft/min

Surviving Example

USAAF 42-94549 – Pima Air and Space Museum

Howard C-70/GH-2 Nightingale

Ben Howard was a prolific designer of small, fast sport airplanes in the early and mid-1930s in his DGA (Damned Good Airplanes) series. After his tiny single-seat DGA-3 "Pete" and twin DGA-4 "Ike" and "Mike", he built a sturdy four-seater, the DGA-6 "Mr. Mulligan". When it was flown to victory in the 1935 Bendix and Thompson Trophy Races, he was faced with the sudden demand for a fast, comfortable, multi-seat touring airplane and responded with his DGA-7 with a larger wing, but otherwise quite similar to the racer.

After making it available with a variety of engines and other equipment as the DGA-8 through -12, he moved on to the definitive version, the DGA-15, which would cruise as fast as 170mph. The demand, despite the continuing effects of the Depression, was surprisingly strong, 80 being sold of all the four-seat high-wing models by the time of America's entry into World War II.

Upon the approach of war, the USAAF had seen the need for a reliable, fast single-engined airplane that would carry a large payload and could be acquired quickly. The Howard DGA-8 through 15 filled the bill and 20 of them were acquired from their private owners and designated UC-70, and UC-70A through D.

Obviously convinced the sporty Howard fitted its needs even more so, the U.S. Navy gave the small Howard Aircraft Co. an order for more than 500 airplanes. A second factory in the suburbs of Chicago was built expressly for this purpose. The U.S. Navy airplanes were designated GH-1 as a VIP transport, GH-2 as a flying ambulance, and NH-1 for an instrument trainer.

After the war, those Howards still in working order were sold on the war surplus market and resumed their civilian roles. Today, they are prized as vintage airplanes that can compete with many modern factory-built types, thanks to their load-carrying capacity and their speed.

Specifications

Length: 25ft 8in
Wingspan: 38ft 0in
Height: 8ft 5in
Wing area: 210 sq ft
Empty weight: 2,700lb
Maximum speed: 200mph
Maximum range: 1,250 miles
Service ceiling: 21,000ft
Rate of climb: 1,800ft/min

Surviving Examples

(civil DGA-15) – private

Boeing C-75 (Stratoliner)

Cabin pressurization was one of the great advances in airline history. It enabled airliners to fly with greater comfort above most of the weather that had long plagued them. It resulted also in operations at much greater speed and efficiency, as aerodynamic drag dropped when the air became thinner, but engine power was maintained with supercharging.

The techniques and equipment needed to maintain pressurization were developed by the U.S. Army Air Corps, flying the experimental XC-35 version of the Lockheed Electra twin-engined transport in the late 1930s. The first production airliner to use this was Boeing's Model 307 Stratoliner, which made its first flight in late 1938. It combined the wings, tail, engines and landing gear of an early

B-17C bomber, with a fuselage having a large circular cross-section to make pressurizing possible.

Boeing built just 10 Stratoliners, the first of which crashed on an early test flight. Five went to TWA, three to TWA and one to Howard Hughes for his personal use. The TWA airplanes were flown between New York and Los Angeles and then sold to the USAAF. They were then modified into C-75s with the removal of the pressurization gear and the addition of long-range fuel tanks. While the PanAm airplanes were used on Central and South American routes, the TWA airplanes and their civilian pilots carried high-value government and military passengers and cargo across the Atlantic Ocean in the first such service.

With newer airplanes taking over the long-distance routes, the TWA airplanes were returned to Boeing in late 1944 and updated with B-17G wings, horizontal tails and engines. Returned to airline service, they continued to carry passengers until 1951, when they were sold to a series of small airlines which operated some of them as late as 1974.

The sole surviving example, one of PanAm's, flew with several little-known airlines until acquired by the government of Haiti for Dictator Duvalier. It was eventually located and added to the vast collection of the U.S. National Air & Space Museum, restored by Boeing and flown to Washington's Dulles International Airport, where it is on display.

Specifications

Length: 74ft 4in
Wingspan: 107ft 3in
Height: 20ft 9in
Wing area: 1,486 sq ft

Empty weight: 30,300lb
Maximum speed: 246mph @ 17,300ft
Maximum range: 2,700 miles
Service ceiling: 26,200ft

Surviving Example

NC-19903 – U.S. National Air & Space Museum

Cessna C-78/JRC Bobcat/Crane

Prior to 1939, the Cessna Airplane Co. had built little other than single-engine, high-wing personal airplanes, most memorably the slick Airmaster. Its first venture into the multi-engine arena was the T-50, aimed at those who wanted twin-engine performance at a lower cost than the Twin Beech. To use non-strategic materials, the airplane had wooden wings and tail, and its fuselage was wood-covered. This led directly to the permanent nick-name of the "Bamboo Bomber".

Before much of a market for the T-50 could be developed, the USAAC decided it would make a good airplane for student pilots who had been trained in single-engined airplanes, to learn the complexities of multi-engined flying. Thus the T-50 became the AT-8, and then with the switch from 295hp Lycoming radial engines to 245hp Jacobs radials, the AT-17 was born. Only 33 of the AT-8 were built before large-scale production began on the AT-17, of which 1,200 were built, starting in 1942.

The Army then saw the simple wooden Bobcat as a possible utility transport, and so 465 AT-17B's were re-designated C-78s and soon UC-78s. Some 65 were transferred to the U.S. Navy as the JRC-1. By the time the line was shut down late in the war, more than 4,400 had been built, including 820 as the Crane Mk.I for the Royal Canadian Air Force to use in the British Commonwealth Air Training Plan.

Many Cessna twins were licensed by the CAA and sold to small commercial operators. Their wooden construction, however, required excessive maintenance, and their usefulness soon faded as newer, all-metal airplanes took their place. Today, a few dozen are flown as restored vintage airplanes.

Specifications

Length: 32ft 9in
Wingspan: 41ft 11in
Height: 9ft 11in

Empty weight: 3,500lb
Maximum speed: 195mph
Maximum range: 750 miles
Service ceiling: 22,000ft

Surviving Examples

C-78
Canadian National Air Museum

UC-78A
Civil SP-GLC – Polish Air Museum-Krakow

UC-78B
USAAF 42-39162 – Pima Air and Space Museum
USAAF 42-71626– National Museum of the U.S. Air Force

JRC-1
U.S. National Museum of Naval Aviation

Fairchild C-82/R4Q Packet

Thousands of Douglas C-47s and Curtiss C-46s established new standards for military air transport systems, lugging uncounted millions of pounds of cargo and tens of thousands of troops in every combat area of World War II. But they could hardly have been the ultimate transport airplanes. With the pressure of war pushing them to do better and faster, the aircraft manufacturing industry had developed innovative advances in power, structures, and aerodynamics that could not be incorporated into existing designs and therefore required entirely new airplanes.

Fairchild Aircraft, which was known up to this point mainly for its single-engined primary trainers, had bigger ideas, the first of which was a novel twin-boom design for an airplane to replace the major types long in use. The C-82 Packet prototype left the ground for the first time in September 1944. Despite having a pair of 2,100hp Pratt & Whitney R-2800 Double Wasp engines, it was considered to be underpowered.

Nevertheless, an order for 200 of the C-82A improved version of the cargo planes was placed by the USAAF, along with 53 more designated R4Q for the U.S. Navy. None was delivered before the war ended in August 1945, but as the prototype had flown during the war, it qualifies for this book. Orders were then placed with North American Aviation for almost 700 of the C-82N, which was almost a prototype for the future C-119, but were canceled right after V-J Day, with only three having been built.

The C-82B then became the C-119 (U.S. Navy R4Q) Flying Boxcar, of which more than 1,100 were built in large numbers after the war and served for many years as a standard cargo and personnel transport.

Specifications

Length: 77ft 1in
Wingspan: 106ft 6in
Height: 26ft 4in
Wing area: 1,400 sq ft
Empty weight: 32,500lb
Maximum speed: 248mph
Maximum range: 3,875 miles
Service ceiling: 21,200ft
Rate of climb: 950ft/min

Surviving Examples

C-82A

USAAF 44-23006 – Pima Air and Space Museum
USAF 48-0574 – McChord Air Museum, Takoma, Washington
USAF 48-0581 – U.S. National Museum of the U.S. Air Force

Budd XC-93/RB-1 Conestoga

America, during World War II, experienced shortages of rubber and various metals, that of aluminum being potentially the most serious, had it developed as feared. While the concern existed, many efforts were considered that would have employed substitute materials, from plywood to stainless steel to early forms of plastic.

As aircraft were the greatest consumers of aluminum, the Budd Co. proposed building a transport in which aluminum was replaced with stainless steel: the RB-1 Conestoga. Had it worked, and had the shortage come to pass, this airplane might have made history. As matters transpired, the shortage never materialized, and the novel flying machine built from the non-strategic metal proved of limited utility.

Maybe the fault lay in the choice of manufacturers. The Budd Co. had a good reputation in stainless steel fabrication, and had produced high quality railroad cars, as well as bus, truck and auto bodies using its proprietary shot-welding process. And while many companies had managed to overcome the problems of transitioning from peacetime manufacturing of common goods to making tanks and cannon, not all of them did so quickly enough.

The first Conestoga flew in October 1943, when its rival C-47 and C-46 were coming off the assembly lines by the hundreds. While it could break ground with a full load in less than 1,000 feet, its range was disappointing due to greater than expected fuel consumption. At a weight considerably more than the C-47, which had already assumed the role as the military's standard, it was underpowered and would be more so when its operations included the frequent need to break the rules covering maximum permissible take-off weight.

The USAAF soon canceled its order for 600 C-93s, and the U.S. Navy accepted only 17 RB-1s and retired all of those by early 1945. The Conestoga had a very short life in military service, and few pilots and mechanics had any direct experience with the type. Perhaps if it had been needed, or if some or all of its problems could have been solved, things might have been different. As it was, the C-47, and to a lesser extent the C-46, had established such

fine reputations that the C-93 really didn't stand much of a chance to prove itself.

Specifications

Length: 68ft 0in
Wingspan: 100ft 0in
Height: 31ft 9in
Wing area: 1,400 sq ft
Empty weight: 20,150lb
Maximum speed: 197mph
Maximum range: 700 miles

Surviving Example

RB-1
BuAer 39307– Pima Air and Space Museum

Boeing C-97 Stratocruiser

Many of the most successful bombers of World War II were modified into cargo and/or troop-carrying airplanes, though with varying degrees of success. Not even the superbly streamlined Boeing B-29 was immune to a process of conversion that may have spoiled its visual symmetry, but ultimately resulted in the first purpose-built flying tanker for mid-air refueling.

The first C-97 consisted of a large upper fuselage atop a standard B-29 fuselage, with wings that would be used in the B-50 advanced development of the XB-44, which, in turn was a B-29 with larger engines. The XC-97 flew for the first time in November 1944, powered by four 2,200hp, 18-cylinder Wright R-3350 engines. The most obvious difference was the rear fuselage ramp which was exposed when clamshell doors were opened only when the airplane was on the ground.

As a demonstration of its speed and range, the XC-97 was flown 2,325 miles from its home in Seattle, Washington, to Washington, DC, in just over six hours for an average speed of 383mph with a payload of 20,000lb

Production models, the first of which was not delivered until well after the end of World War II, in 1947, were powered by the huge 28-cylinder, 3,500hp Pratt & Whitney R-4360 Wasp Major engine. The great majority – 815 – were built as KC-97 flying tankers for mid-air refueling, while only some 60 were C-97 cargo transports.

Specifications

Length: 110ft 4in
Wingspan: 141ft 3in
Height: 38ft 3in
Wing area: 1,734 sq ft
Empty weight: 82,500lb
Maximum speed: 375mph
Maximum range: 4,950 miles
Service ceiling: 35,000ft
Maximum load: 37,500lb

Surviving Examples

Post-war C-97G
USAF 52-898 – Chanute Aerospace Museum, Illinois
USAF 52-2626 – Pima Air and Space Museum
USAF 53-0272 – Milestones of Flight Museum, Fox Field, Lancaster, California

Martin JRM-1 Mars

By the early 1930s aviation was beginning to stretch its wings, having experienced enough long-range record flights to see that its future lay in carrying ever-heavier loads on ever-longer flights. Since long paved runways were only beginning to enter use, almost all the schemes involved flying boats, there being no other way to get heavy flying machines into the air.

The major industrial nations – Great Britain, the U.S.A., France and the emerging Nazi Germany – were aiming at larger and larger flying boats for long over-water routes. Shorts, Sikorsky, Consolidated, Boeing, Martin, Blohm & Voss, and others had design projects for four- and six-engined behemoths that would tax the creativity of aeronautical engineers for years to come.

In 1936, the U.S. Navy went shopping for a very long range flying boat that could cover vast distances in the Pacific and Atlantic Oceans with sufficient bomb loads to make them effective weapons against ships of future enemies. In the U.S.A, the Glenn L. Martin Co. was proceeding with its PBM Mariner twin-engined flying boat in response to a 1936 order. Just two years later, a new contract was issued for a much larger craft, to be known at first as the XPB2M-1.

It would use four 2,000hp Wright R-3350 Duplex Cyclone engines, still under development themselves, having been flown on the XB-19 very heavy bomber. With a wingspan of 200 feet and gross weight of 140,000lb, the prototype which was rolled (splashed?) out in 1939 was as large as anything that had yet taken flight. By now, however, its function had been changed from patrol-bomber to cargo transport.

Due to an accident during test runs, which required extensive repairs, it had become the XPB2M-1R when all offensive weapons had been removed. It was finally flown in July 1942, and within five months was making long-distance flights as far as 4,600 miles, and shorter runs with payloads of up to 30,000lb

While the Mars was demonstrating the predicted performance of large flying boats, the rapid technological progress of wartime was making her obsolete. More and more hard-surface runways were enabling large, heavy landplanes equipped with variable-pitch propellers to operate almost anywhere, while flying boats were limited to locations having long stretches of open water.

In 1944 the U.S. Navy ordered 20 of the modified (a single large vertical tail replaced the twin rudders) to become the JRM Mars, which was especially set up for the hauling of freight. After the first production boat was delivered in the summer of 1945, the end of the war resulted in all but five being canceled. With the original Wright engines continuing to have mechanical problems, all the remaining Mars were re-fitted with 3,000hp Pratt & Whitney R-4360 engines.

Post-war operations displayed the JRM's load-carrying ability, with take-off weights of 165,000lb, and loads of 38,000lb fairly standard. But the hand writing was on the wall: large piston-engined landplanes and then jets were doing more with less, so the remaining Mars were used for fire-fighting in Canada.

Specifications

Length: 117ft 3in
Wingspan: 200ft 0in
Height: 38ft 5in
Wing area: 3,686 sq ft
Empty weight: 75,575lb
Maximum speed: 221mph
Service ceiling: 14,600ft
Maximum load: 32,000lb

Surviving Examples

BuAer 76820 "Phillipine Mars" – Sproat Lake, British Columbia, Canada
BuAer 76823 "Hawaii Mars II" – Sproat Lake

Great Britain

dH.89A Dominie

The civil Dragon Rapide (the "Dragon" was later dropped) was the leading British commuter airliner of the mid and late-1930s. Not even its proliferation of wing struts and wires and bulky landing gear fairings played much of a role in the limited speed necessary to travel the 30- and 40-mile legs around its relatively small nation. Scores of them carried loads of 6–10 passengers up and down from one small airfield to the next.

When it came time for the RAF to start acquiring new airplanes for coastal reconnaissance, the Rapide lost out to the Avro Anson, but attracted a contract in early 1939 for communications purposes, which covers a variety of functions. It became a radio trainer at

about the same time and was soon ferrying ferry pilots of the Air Transport Auxiliary from one airfield to another.

What was soon to be called the Dominie by the RAF was a quite basic airplane with fabric covering its mainly plywood structure. Power was provided by a pair of 200hp deHavilland Gipsy Queen inline engines. With a gracefully tapered wings having a somewhat high aspect ratio of almost 7:1, it could operate off very short grass runways.

The first Rapide flew in April 1934 and demonstrated good flying qualities and few bad habits. They were soon a common sight along the developing airway system of the British Isles. More than 200 were built before the war started in 1939, with many finding their way around Europe.

Many of the British-owned Rapides became Dominies when impressed during the war, and were joined by more than 500 built expressly for the RAF and a few for the Fleet Air Arm. Of the total of 731 built as both civil and military airplanes, only 186 came from the deHavilland factory, the great bulk having been farmed out to the Brush Coachworks.

After the war, many found their way back into short-haul commercial uses, and some can still be seen in outlying areas of the British Isles.

Specifications

Length: 34ft 6in
Wingspan: 48ft 0in
Height: 10ft 3in
Wing area: 340 sq ft
Empty weight: 3,230lb
Maximum speed: 157mph

Maximum range: 575 miles
Service ceiling: 16,700ft
Rate of climb: 867ft/min

Surviving Examples

RAF HG691 (G-AYIR) – Imperial War Museum, Duxford (available for joy rides)
RAF X7344 (G-AGJG) – Imperial War Museum, Duxford
RAF X7454 – National Museum of the U.S. Air Force
G-ADAH – Museum of Science and Industry, Manchester
G-AGSN – Jet Heritage Collection, Bournemouth, Dorset
G-AKDW – deHavilland Heritage Museum
PP-VAN – Brazilian Aerospace Museum, Rio de Janiero

Avro York

When it flew overhead it was barely distinguishable from the mighty Lancaster heavy bomber, of which it was a direct descendant. The wings were Lancaster, as were the engines and the tail, though a third vertical tail was added to deal with minor instability due to the higher, slab-sided fuselage and the slightly longer nose. The prototype flew in July 1942. Seen from the side, it had a markedly different profile, as well as a long line of round passenger windows

The second pre-production York to be completed, in March 1943, was an airborne conference room, carrying high-ranking government and military officials to important meetings. Others followed slowly, as large-scale construction of Lancasters took precedence. The first squadron was not completed until 1945, as the flow of C-47 and C-54s was carrying the load.

The real era of the York began shortly after the war ended, when seven full squadrons took part in the emergency Berlin air lift, when they carried more than 200,000 tons of supplies, ranging from food to coal, to a city cut off by the occupying Soviets.

Civilian use of the York began in early 1944 with a single airplane used temporarily by the RAF to serve on the England to India run. It had been built for British Overseas Airways Corporation (BOAC) and was operated by the RAF's Transport Command.

With some 50 built for airline use, and others converted after the war, they flew to such faraway parts as South Africa, the Caribbean and South America, with passengers until 1949 and then freight until 1957. A few were sold off to smaller airlines which operated Yorks as late as 1964. With the exception of the prototype, which was converted to Bristol Hercules radial engines late in its life, all were powered by four 1,300hp Rolls Royce Merlin XX V-12s.

Specifications

Length: 78ft 6in
Wingspan: 102ft 0in
Height: 16ft 6in
Wing area: 1,297 sq ft
Empty weight: 40,000lb
Maximum speed: 298mph
Maximum range: 3,000 miles
Service ceiling: 23,000ft
Maximum payload: 20,000lb

Surviving Examples

Mk. C.1
RAF MW232 – Imperial War Museum, Duxford as G-ANTK
RAF TS798 – RAF-Museum, Cosford as G-AGNV

Union of Soviet Socialist Republics

Lisunov Li-2/C-47

With no modern airliners of its own in its foreseeable future, the Soviet government arranged to build Douglas DC-3s on license, and even sent an engineer to study Douglas manufacturing methods in expectation of building its own fleet of what was rapidly becoming the world's standard. After this engineer was arrested and relocated to a Soviet prison camp along with many other critically important aviation industry specialists, he was replaced for two years in California by Boris Lisunov.

Due to the need to change all the Imperial measurements on hundreds of drawings to Metric, and then specify slightly larger sizes and greater thicknesses for the less sophisticated original materials the Soviets had to replace them with, almost every part was changed to some extent. This resulted in a weight increase of at least 500lb, which was not helped by the change to the less powerful Shevtsov Ash-62 engine. The new engine was a development of the American Wright R-1820, while the DC-3/C-47 used two 1,200hp Pratt & Whitney R-1830s.

On the airframe, which from a distance looked exactly like a C-47, the passenger door was moved to the right side, and replaced on the left with a cargo door. Once the Germans invaded the U.S.S.R. in 1941, many civilian Li-2 airliners found themselves with top turrets equipped at first with a single .30 cal. machine gun and then with a single .50 cal., along with bomb racks and provisions for skis in place of the wheels for use in the frigid northern areas of that vast nation.

While relatively few Li-2s had been built as airliners, a large government factory near Moscow began turning the military version out in quantity. Later, in the face of the German advance toward Moscow, the factory was relocated far to the East. As the number of Red DC-3s grew, so did the variety of uses to which they were put. Some simply carried troops, including airborne soldiers. Others became long-range bombers or flying ambulances. They dropped supplies to cut-off partisan groups, as well as hundreds of thousands trapped during the siege of Leningrad.

Like the original DC-3, the Li-2 soldiered on past the retirement of its contemporaries. Some were in the service of the Chinese and Vietnamese into the 1980s, and in Eastern European airlines for almost as long

By the end of the war, production had topped 2,200 airplanes. At the end of Soviet production in 1954, that had grown considerably. While estimates vary greatly, the lowest are near 5,000 and the highest exceed 6,000. Regardless, it is the greatest total production of a foreign designed airplane in Soviet history.

Specifications

Length: 64ft 5in
Wingspan: 94ft 6in
Wing area: 983 sq ft
Empty weight: 17,485lb
Maximum speed: 186mph
Maximum range: 1,500 miles
Service ceiling: 18,370 ft

Surviving Examples

Hungarian AF 18433209 – may still be flying at Budaors, Hungary
Polish AF 18436204 – Polish Air Museum, Krakow

Germany

Junkers Ju.52

The Luftwaffe had its Ju.52; the Allies had their C-47. They came from different eras and looked the part. But their performance did not differ that much, and they served their multiple roles with honor and verve.

The Ju.52 first flew in October 1930 as the prototype of a single-engined descendant of a long line of pioneering all-metal airliners. However, after only a few had been built, it was recognized that one engine of the size then available would not carry the desired loads. This resulted in the Ju.52/3m, the first of which flew in March 1932, powered by three 550hp American Pratt & Whitney R-1690 Hornet engines.

The airplane was a success, and by the time it had entered series production, most used a license-built Hornet called the BMW 132 which, with improvements, was rated at 770hp. Export sales helped fill the order book, with a variety of engines in use, including the 600hp P&W R-1340 Wasp, the 775hp Bristol Pegasus VI and on one occasion a single 880hp Rolls Royce Buzzard V-12.

The Ju.52s first departure from the airliner role came during the Spanish Civil War, when several of the bomber version were used effectively against undefended civilian targets, including during the historic destruction of Guernica in 1937. Production of this type was limited, and when Ju.52s dropped bombs on Warsaw, Poland, at the start of World War II, they were transports hurriedly adapted for the role.

Aside from the routine carriage of men and cargo, they made the headlines during the Battle of Crete in 1941 by successfully dropping a large number of paratroops. As the war wore on, the Ju.52s lack of speed made it an easy target for Allied fighters, especially when the German transport was used in large formations. Heavy fighter protection was necessary to assure completion of vital missions, such as the supply of Wehrmacht troops at Stalingrad. When Rommel's Afrika Korps had been pushed back by Montgomery's 8th Army to a last-ditch stand in Libya, the evacuation of soldiers was attempted by formations of Ju.52s, with dozens being shot down and their passengers killed.

Despite its lack of performance, the Ju.52 proved amenable to new uses requiring extensive modifications. Equipped with two large floats, they operated from the fjords during the fighting in Norway in the early part of the war, as well as later in the Mediterranean.

When the war ended, the Ju.52 returned to service as an airliner, there being a greater need than the limited supply of ex-military machines could meet. They served with Scandinavian and Swiss Air, as well as air forces in Europe, South Africa and South America. The Swiss Air Force operated them as late as the 1980s. The total manufactured was almost 5,000.

Specifications

Length: 62ft 0in
Wingspan: 95ft 10in
Height: 14ft 10in
Wing area: 1,190 sq ft
Maximum speed: 165mph
Maximum range: 540 miles
Service ceiling: 18,000ft
Time to climb: 10,000ft in 17:00

Surviving Examples

Ju.52/3m
c/n 4043 – National Aeronautical Museum, Buenos Aires, Argentina
civil D-CDLH – Lufthansa, Germany

Ju.52/g3e
Luftwaffe 106/6306 – Norwegian National Aviation Museum, Bodoe

Ju.52/g4e
c/n 6309 – Junkers Museum, Dessau, Germany
Swiss AF – Zubendorf, near Zurich, Switzerland

Ju.52/g7e
c/n 6134 – Royal Army Museum, Brussels, Belgium

Amiot AAC.1
c/n 6316 "4V+GH" – Imperial War Museum, Duxford

CASA 352L
Spain T.2B-211 – Museo del Aire, Cuatro Vientos
Spain T.2B-244 – National Museum of the U.S. Air Force
Spain T.2B-255 – U.S. National Air & Space Museum
Spain T.2B-272 – RAF Museum, Cosford

Chapter 2

Trainers

The primary trainer was the first airplane which most student military pilots ever flew. As such, its design was critical, for there was little time for an instructor to decide which of his students had the potential for bigger and better things, and which were destined to become infantrymen and ordinary seamen. A primary trainer had to be easy to fly, and yet mentally and physically challenging enough to bring out the innate skills needed to cope with the increasing power and complexity of basic and advanced trainers, and then, with only a hundred of so hours of flight time, combat airplanes.

United States of America

Boeing Stearman PT-13/PT-17/PT-18/PT-27/N2S Kaydet
The U.S. Army Air Corps and Navy had been doing their best to teach would-be pilots on airplanes they had bought in the early 1930s, when war seemed a very remote possibility. When the war clouds began to gather, it became obvious that the Army and Navy might need a lot of new pilots in a hurry, and so the word went out that a new primary trainer was in order.

The first of the new generation was the Navy's NS-1, built as a private venture by Lloyd Stearman's small company, which became a subsidiary of Boeing in 1934. It bore a strong resemblance to the original Stearman PT-9, built in limited numbers in 1932, and to subsequent trainers from Consolidated in the same time period. With a little more power from its 220hp Lycoming R-680 radial engine, the PT-13 became the new standard of Army trainers. By the time it was replaced by the Army's Stearman PT-17 and the Navy's N2S in 1940, almost 700 had had been delivered.

The flow of rookie pilots was soon being measured by the tens of thousands, and many of the new trainers were soon being bent and broken by those succumbing to the pressures of flight training.

The PT-17 was built by Boeing-Stearman, yet still referred to as a Stearman. Between 1940 and 1942, almost 10,000 were built, most with 220hp Continental R-670 radial engines.

At the same time, 150 others were built with 225hp Jacobs R-755 engines, and still more – 300 – were built as PT-27s, with closed canopies. All of these variants were virtually interchangeable, having the same dimensions and performance, including several thousand delivered to the U.S. Navy.

After serving the military of many countries as the first airplane in which World War II pilots received formal instruction, they continued on. One of the most popular types declared as surplus at the end of the war, it was in demand for agricultural duties and was modified with bins for chemicals to be sprayed on crops, and as a sport plane.

Despite its mixed construction of fabric-covered wooden wings and solid steel tube fuselage structure, much of which was subject to the corrosive effects of some of the chemicals it carried, many have survived to this day. Some as ag-planes, which remain cheaper to operate than the newer, designed-for-the purpose types, and as sport airplanes whose aerobatic capabilities make them excellent air show performers.

Specifications

Length: 25ft 0in
Wingspan: 32ft 2in
Height: 9ft 2in
Wing area: 297 sq ft
Empty weight: 1,935lb
Maximum speed: 125mph
Maximum range: 500 miles

Service ceiling: 11,200ft
Rate of climb: 840ft/min

Surviving Examples

PT-13D
USAAF 42-16388 (ex-PT-17) – March Field Air Museum
USAAF 42-17800 – National Museum of the U.S. Air Force
USAAF 42-17786 composite – Imperial War Museum, Duxford
USAAF m/s 75-3412 – Kalamazoo Air Zoo, Michigan

PT-17
USAAF 41-8860 – Musee de l'Air
USAAF 41-8882 – Pima Air and Space Museum

N2S-3
USN BuAer 05369– U.S. National Museum of Naval Aviation Fighter Factory

N2S-4
c/n 75-2326 – U.S. National Museum of Naval Aviation

N2S-5
U.S. National Museum of Naval Aviation
USAAF 42-17023 – U.S. National Air & Space Museum

Ryan PT-16/PT-20/PT-21/PT-22/NR Recruit

With the day of the military biplane passing, it was inevitable that even primary trainers meant to replace the Stearman PT-1 etc would have to be monoplanes, preferably with cantilever (internally-

braced) wings if they were to give their pilots realistic experience. The first of these to equip U.S. Army and Navy training units were Ryan PT-16s, a few of which were built as early as 1939.

The Ryan began life as the STA, one of the most attractive personal airplanes of the 1930s. With its Menasco inline engine, low-drag tandem windshields and neatly faired landing gear, it was the classic aerial sports car, despite the collection of struts and wires holding its wings in place.

The Army Air Corps soon discovered that the Menasco engine lacked the reliability demanded for an airplane whose pilots lacked experience and were under severe pressure to learn quickly or be faced with dismissal. The product of an engine builder who had earned a good reputation building racing engines was replaced with a rough-sounding 5-cylinder Kinner R-440 radial. The concurrent removal of the engine cowling and landing gear

fairings turned it into a homely, noisy airplane that managed to do the job demanded by a military that cared little for aeronautical niceties.

The result was the PT-20, of which only 30 were built, and then the PT-21 (100 built) and then the main PT-22 version, of which more than 1,000 came off the assembly line. Including those built for the U.S. Navy and those exported to the Netherlands East Indies and the Royal Australian Air Force, the final total was more than 1,500.

Specifications

Length: 21ft 5in
Wingspan: 30ft 0in
Height: 9ft 2in

Wing area: 124 sq ft
Empty weight: 1,080lb
Maximum speed: 125mph
Maximum range: 365 miles
Service ceiling: 17,200ft
Rate of climb: 800ft/min

Surviving Examples

YPT-16
National Museum of the U.S. Air Force

PT-22
USAAC 41-15550 – Palm Springs (California) Air Museum
USAAC 41-15721 – National Museum of the U.S. Air Force
USAAC 41-15736 – Pima Air and Space Museum

NR-1
U.S. National Museum of Naval Aviation

Fairchild PT-19/PT-23/PT-26 Cornell

As the speeds of operational combat airplanes increased, there was a need for a primary trainer that would better prepare fledgling pilots, while retaining as much of their easy flying characteristics as possible. This led to the PT-19 series with its 200hp Fairchild Ranger air-cooled engine that gave it a speed some 10mph higher than the PT-17 biplane or the PT-22.

While its fuselage was built up from welded steel tubes, most of the remainder was wood, which led to serious problems. The many training fields in Florida exposed the Fairchilds to the salty

sea air which rotted their structures and forced the replacement of major components at such frequency that the later production airplanes had all-metal wing structures.

The prototype of the mass-produced trainer was Fairchild's privately financed M-62, which was entered in the U.S. Army's 1939 primary trainer competition along with 17 others, including the popular Waco UPF-7 sport airplane and the Meyers OTW. The three that were selected were those described in this sub-section.

The first PT-19s to come out of the factory were from a batch of 275 powered by the 175hp, six-cylinder inline Ranger L-440-1 engine. Soon they were replaced by the PT-19A with a 200hp version of the same engine, and almost 3,200 were built, along with 900 PT-19B which had collapsible fabric hoods for the student receiving instruction in instrument flying.

Fairchild, which had never before built anything in such quantities, found itself unable to supply sufficient engines to meet the needs of its own airplanes. This led to installation of the seven-cylinder, 220hp Continental R-670 radial engine in what became the PT-23. That, in turn, required a major widening of the front fuselage, which had been quite narrow when fitted with an inline engine.

Expansion of training facilities in Canada required further modifications, the most obvious of which was the installation of a closed canopy to keep out the cold winds when flying more than 1,000 miles north of most USAAF training bases in the southern U.S.A. The resulting PT-26 reverted to the Ranger engine. The Canadians called the type the Cornell, which was later adopted for all the airplanes built in the PT-19/PT-23/PT-26 series.

Like its brother primary trainers, the Fairchilds proved financially appealing to recently demobilized U.S. Army and Navy pilots, and so several hundred soon joined the civil register. Now, more than a half century later, they can be seen in their bright blue-and-yellow color schemes at many fly-ins and air shows.

Specifications

Length: 27ft 8in
Wingspan: 35ft 11in
Height: 7ft 9in
Wing area: 200 sq ft
Loaded weight: 2,450lb
Maximum speed: 124mph
Maximum range: 480 miles
Service ceiling: 16,000ft
Rate of climb: 650ft/min

Surviving Examples

PT-19A
National Museum of the U.S. Air Force
USAAC 41-14675 – Pima Air and Space Museum
USAAF 42-91659 – National Museum of the U.S. Air Force
USAAF 43-33842 – U.S. National Air & Space Museum

PT-19B
USAAF 43-5598 – March Field Air Museum
Civil N61013 – Experimental Aircraft Association

PT-26
Planes of Fame
Cornell III – Canadian Aviation & Space Museum

PT-26B
s/n 10738– Canadian National Aviation Museum

Vultee BT-13/BT-15/SNV Valiant

Once a young aviator had shown that he was capable of taking off, flying, navigating and then landing without breaking major parts of his airplane or himself, he was deemed ready for the next step: basic flight training. Unlike the primary training phase in which three distinct types were used in quantity, there was only a single significant basic trainer.

The demands on the basic trainer were considerably greater than on the primary trainer, as it had to prepare the student for not only more complicated and high-performance advanced trainers, but also for multi-engined airplanes, which many of them would

soon be flying. The first attempt by Vultee reflected this, the private venture V-51 having a 600hp Pratt & Whitney Wasp radial engine, a variable-pitch propeller, hydraulically-operated wing flaps and retractable landing gear.

While this must have been seen as highly desirable, those responsible for selecting new designs decided it was too complicated, too sophisticated and certainly too expensive. The U.S. Army Air Corps was having trouble getting Congress to allocate enough funds to pay its bills, and buying such an airplane would have been seen as extravagant.

Vultee wisely toned down its next proposal, for a 1939 trainer competition, which it lost to North American Aviation's BC-2, which was a simplified predecessor to the AT-6 which would soon dominate the next phase of training. The Army wisely ordered

the prototype of Vultee's BC-51, which became the improved and more realistic VF-54. That, in turn, evolved into the BT-13, using a 450hp P&W R-985 Wasp Jr.

Two hundred BT-13s were ordered in mid-1939. Deliveries began in 1940 and reached a total of more than 6,400 as training fields began to pop up all over the southern U.S.A., where the weather permitted flying almost every day. The Navy jumped on the bandwagon, ordering 1,150 BT-13As as SNV-1s, and 650 BT-13Bs as SNV-2Bs. Tens of thousands of young men poured through the system, accumulating a few dozen hours and enough proficiency to qualify them for the next stage.

In 1942, Pratt & Whitney's ability to meet the mushrooming demand for its increasingly popular Wasp Jr, and to prepare for the production of the soon-to-be-standard R-2800, was under considerable strain, Vultee saw the need to build a variation of the BT-13 using the more readily available Wright R-975, which produced the same power. This was the BT-15, of which some 1,700 were built.

Such was the usefulness of the Vultee trainer that only one other type was ordered during World War II. North American's BT-14, of which just 250 were built, was a development of its late-1930s BT-9. It might have served better as a preparation for the AT-6, but Vultee's airplane was solidly established.

All through its military career it was officially known as the "Valiant", at least on paper. Among those who flew them, it was the "Vibrator", thanks to its pronounced shake indicating an impending stall. No doubt this was appreciated by both students and instructors. The hundreds, of more than 11,000 built, that were sold as surplus after the war, were unanimously called by this affectionate name.

Specifications

Length: 28ft 10in
Wingspan: 42ft 0in
Height: 11ft 6in
Wing area: 239 sq ft
Empty weight: 3,375lb
Maximum speed: 180mph
Maximum range: 725 miles
Service ceiling: 21,650ft
Rate of climb: 770ft/min

Surviving Examples

BT-13A
USAAF 41-1306 – March Field Air Museum
USAAF 41-22124 – U.S. National Air & Space Museum
USAAF 42-42353 – Pima Air and Space Museum

BT-13B
USAAF 42-90629 – National Museum of the U.S. Air Force

SNV-1
BuAer 60828 – U.S. National Museum of Naval Aviation

SNV-2
s/n 79-1420 – Cavanaugh Flight Museum, Texas

North American BT-9/BT-14 Yale

From its inception as an airframe producer in 1934 until the approach of World War II, North American Aviation was a little-known builder of training airplanes for mainly small air forces. It soon became one of the most important airplane manufacturers in the world.

Its first successful product was the BT-9 basic trainer, a development of the NA-16, the first of which flew in 1936. The thinking behind it revealed great foresight, as even today, it looks like an AT-6 Texan/Harvard except for its non-retracting landing gear. The control surfaces and much of the fuselage were fabric covered, while everything else was metal. Power was rated at 400hp from a Wright R-975 Whirlwind.

The U.S. Army Air Corps bought a total of 199, with the first being delivered in 1936, as development and proving tasks were much simpler in those days than they are in today's ultra high-tech world. After 42 were built, the BT-9A went into production with a pair of .30 cal. machine guns. After 40 of those were delivered, the BT-9B followed as a slightly modified BT-9, starting in 1937. Ninety-seven BT-9Cs were built to the same Specifications, bringing the total to 199. The U.S. Navy, not to be out-done, ordered 40 versions called the NJ-1 and with the bigger 600hp Pratt & Whitney R-1340 radial engine.

Export sales accounted for a major part of North American's business in the 1930s, with a batch of BT-9s it called the NA-57, sold to France, of which 30 were for the French Navy. When France capitulated to the Germans in 1940, the Luftwaffe took the North American trainers and painted swastikas on their tails. Another 137 of the NA-16-4M were built on license by SAAB in Sweden and called the Sk 14.

Empty weight: 3,314lb
Maximum speed: 170mph
Maximum range: 880 miles
Service ceiling: 19,750ft

Surviving Examples

BT-9C
Honduran Air Force tail number 21 – NA-16 at Museum of the Air

BT-14A (NA-64)
RCAF 3450 – National Museum of the U.S. Air Force

NA-64
RCAF3350 – Canadian Warplane Heritage Museum
RCAF3397 – Pima Air & Space Museum
RCAF3411 – Canadian Warplane Heritage Museum
RCAF 3430 – Western Canada Aviation Museum, Winnipeg, Manitoba

Beginning in 1940, the assembly line began turning out a total of 251 BT-14s, which were improved BT-9s powered by the highly regarded Pratt & Whitney R-985 Wasp Jr. Of those, 27 became BT-14A's with a de-rated Wasp Jr.

The final version was the export NA-64 Yale, 111 of which were delivered to France before it surrendered in 1940, while the other 119 were for the British, who transferred them to the Royal Canadian Air Force, which used them throughout the war.

All the remaining airplanes are from that order, even the "BT-14" on display in the National Museum of the U.S. Air Force.

Specifications

Length: 28ft 0in
Wingspan: 42ft 0in
Height: 13ft 7in

North American AT-6/SNJ/Harvard/AT-16

With the introduction of the AT-6, the American military (and then others) at last had a trainer worthy of the title, having mildly challenging handling characteristics which gave the rookie pilot a more realistic preparation for what was to come in Mustangs and Thunderbolts.

The original idea had been that a trainer should be a "pussycat" and had extended to the use of Piper J-3 Cubs for many a student airplane driver's first taste of control. The advent of the AT-6 changed this.

The origins of the AT-6 were unmistakable, it resembling the earlier North American BT-9 except for its retractable landing gear. The immediate predecessor of the AT-6 was the BC-1, in the short-lived Basic Combat category. It went into production in 1937, with 180 being built for the U.S. Army Air Corps and 400 for the RAF. Sixteen were slightly modified for the U.S. Navy as SNJ-1s.

Despite the "Combat" implication, they were trainers, and fully recognized as such when the first few BC-1A's became the first AT-6s with the adoption of modified shapes for the wings and vertical tail which stayed with the series for years to come. It was a time when few paid attention to such changes, and so they were considered of little account.

Production of the original AT-6A saw the program achieve major status, with more than 1,500 being built for the Air Force and more as SNJ-3 for the U.S. Navy, with the 600hp Pratt & Whitney R-1340 Wasp engine. An additional 1,500 were manufactured for the Army as the AT-16 and almost 2,500 for the RAF, Fleet Air Arm and RCAF by Norduyn Aircraft, in Canada.

Changes to the electrical system resulted in the AT-6C, of which 3,000 were built for the USAAF, 2,400 as SNJ-4 for the Navy and 725 for the RAF. More modification including an improved hydraulic system and steerable tail wheel led to the AT-6D of which 1,350 became SNJ-5, 3,700 AT-6D and more than 900 as Harvard III for the RAF and FAA.

With more than 15,000 AT-6s, SNJ2 and Harvards delivered, the training of pilots reached its highest level ever, in terms of both quantity and quality. With only accidents and mechanical failures decreasing the supply, these airplanes were used to perfect the skills of hundreds of thousands. After the war, at least 1,500 were sold as surplus, as they offered good performance at far less cost than combat airplanes.

Today, they can be seen at scores of private airfields around the world, and in the annual National Championship Air Races at Reno, Nevada, where there has been a separate class for the series since the late 1960s.

Specifications

Length: 29ft 0in
Wingspan: 42ft 0in
Height: 11ft 8in
Wing area: 254 sq ft
Empty weight: 4,158lb
Maximum speed: 208mph
Maximum range: 730 miles
Service ceiling: 24,000ft

Some Surviving Examples

AT-6B Texan
USAAF 41-17246 – Pima Air and Space Museum

AT-6D
USAAF '44-63221ft – Imperial War Museum, Duxford

SNJ-2
The Fighter Factory

SNJ-4
BuAer 51360 – March Field Air Museum
BuAer 51398 – U.S. National Air & Space Museum, The Fighter Factory

SNJ-5
USAAF (?) 44-86287 – Planes of Fame

SNJ-5C
BuAer 91005 – Kalamazoo Air Zoo, Michigan
U.S. National Museum of Naval Aviation

SNJ-6
U.S. National Museum of Naval Aviation

SNJ-7
BuAer 112943 – Kalamazoo Air Zoo, Michigan

Mk.IIB
"43" – Imperial War Museum, Duxford

Mk.IV
USAF 53-4619 (re-mfd.) – Imperial War Museum, Duxford

Norduyn AT-16
USAAF 42-892 or 42-12479 or 43-13064 – Imperial War Museum, Duxford

Beech AT-7/SNB Navigator and AT-11 Kansan

The Beech 18 in all its many guises was manufactured from 1937 to 1970 as a multi-purpose civil workhorse, as a military transport (C-45) and as a military trainer (AT-7, AT-11 and SNB). They reached the peak of productivity during the war years, when they trained tens of thousands of new pilots to fly and function in twin-engined airplanes.

It began life in 1937 when the first prototype of the civil Model 18 flew, carrying with it Beech's hopes for a small airliner to compete with Lockheed's Electra, which was already becoming established. The 18 suffered from inferior performance to its rival, due in great part to a lack of suitable power. The first airplanes manufactured used the 330hp Jacobs L-6 radial. This was soon replaced by a pair of 350hp Wright R-760, and finally 450hp Pratt & Whitney R-985 Wasp Jr.

Only a few dozen 18s were sold before the war, and then Beech got a big break. Lockheed found itself with all the work it could handle, and so its orders for Electras were transferred to Beech, which charged into mass production for the first time in its short history. The C-45 transport was on its way to success.

With the prospect of thousands of single-engined trainers being turned out by Stearman, Fairchild and Ryan, there was s sudden need for an airplane with two engines to ease pilots into military transports and then twin- and four-engined bombers. The immediate future would require airplanes to train just as many navigators and bombardiers. Beech was ready.

First came the AT-7 Navigator, which began to roll off the assembly lines in 1942 equipped with an astrodome from which novices could learn to shoot the sun and stars. A few were built to operate from floats (AT-7A) while others were specially modified for cold-weather operations (AT-7B). In all, almost 600 AT-7s were built, a few for the RAF.

The major version was the AT-11 Kansan, most of the 1,600 being for bombardier training, which meant using a then-secret Norden bombsight. Others (AT-11A) were specifically for students of the fine art of gunnery and had a single .30 cal. machine guns in the nose and another in a turret atop the fuselage.

The U.S. Navy and Marine Corps received more than 1,100 Beech trainers. The SNB-1, of which 320 were built, was a bombardier

trainer; The SNB-2, of which 510 were built, was a navigator trainer, and the SNB-3, of which 375 were built, was the standard AT-7 with an improved P&W engine.

Almost 4,000 examples of the Beech Model 18 were built as trainers, and were said to have been involved in the education of 90 per cent of some 45,000 bombardiers in the U.S. military. After the war, hundreds of Model 18 derivatives were sold as surplus to military needs, while hundreds more new ones were manufactured to meet the need of small airlines and small corporations as executive transports.

Specifications

Length: 34ft 2in
Wingspan: 47ft 8in
Height: 9ft 8in

Wing area: 349 sq ft
Empty weight: 6,175lb
Maximum speed: 225mph
Maximum range: 1,200 miles
Service ceiling: 26,000ft
Rate of climb: 1,850ft/min

Surviving Examples

AT-7
USAAF 42-2438 – Pima Air and Space Museum
USAAF 43-33316 – Military Aircraft Restoration Society (MAPS), Canton, Ohio, as SNB-2 BuAer 67103

AT-11
USAAC 41-9577 – Pima Air & Space Museum
USAAF 42-37493 – National Museum of the U.S. Air Force

SNB
BuAer 44588 – March Field Aviation Museum

Curtiss-Wright AT-9 Jeep
While the advanced trainers developed from the commercial Beech Model 18 were based on a well-proved design, the AT-9 Jeep was expressly intended for pilots who would soon be flying "hot" airplanes such as the P-38 Lightning and B-25 Mitchell. It had intentionally challenging take-off and landing characteristics which would have to be mastered before a student would be permitted to move on to operational airplanes.

The prototype Jeep had wood wings and extensive fabric covering, all changed to metal before production began. A smaller airplane than either the AT-9 or AT-11, it was nevertheless able to reach speeds near theirs on the power of just two 295hp Lycoming R-680 radial engines.

Total production of the Jeep was almost 800, but none was ever placed on the military surplus market as it was felt that its less-than-ideal stability, along with some other flight characteristics made it a poor airplane for private flyers. Most of those surviving the rough treatment by students were broken up at war's end, with only two known to have survived.

Specifications

Length: 31ft 8in
Wingspan: 40ft 4in
Height: 9ft 10in
Wing area: 233 sq ft
Empty weight: 4,495lb
Maximum speed: 197mph
Maximum range: 750 miles
Service ceiling: 19,000ft
Rate of climb: 10,000ft in 8:35

AT-9
USAAC 41-12150 – National Museum of the U.S. Air Force

AT-9A
USAAF 42-56882 – Pima Air and Space Museum

Beech AT-10 Wichita

The only twin-engined trainer meant expressly for transitioning pilots from single-engined trainers was the relatively little-known Beech AT-10. And unlike the multi-purpose versions of the same company's AT-7, it did not descend from any civil type.

The AT-10 was a minimum size airplane built almost entirely of non-strategic materials, which generally meant wood. Just before and just after America entered the war, there was considerable concern that the supply of available bauxite ore simply would not produce enough aluminum to meet the huge demand of all the airframe factories which were expected to spring up.

As a result, the AT-10 had its entire airframe built from plywood, with the only sheet aluminum being used for the engine cowlings and the cockpit area. Even the fuel tanks were wood, with a covering of neoprene, a synthetic rubber developed by DuPont chemists. Many parts of the AT-10 were sub-contracted out to small furniture makers.

The AT-10 prototype flew for the first time in early 1941, soon crashed and was replaced by a second prototype in July. By the following February, it had been accepted by the USAAF and was in production. The total production by Beech amounted to 1,770 by the time it had been shifted to Globe (later to build the Swift, one of the sportiest of post-war personal airplanes) which built an additional 600.

An estimated half of all USAAF multi-engined pilots received their first experience with complex, retractable landing gear airplanes in the Wichita, and passed on to P-38 and P-61 fighters, and to B-17, B-24, B-25, B-26 and B-29 bombers.

Specifications

Length: 34ft 4in
Wingspan: 44ft 0in
Height: 10ft 4in
Wing area: 298 sq ft
Empty weight: 4,750lb
Maximum speed: 198mph
Maximum range: 770 miles
Service ceiling: 16,900ft
Rate of climb: 10,000 ft in 12:42

Surviving Example

Composite airframe – National Museum of the U.S. Air Force

Republic AT-12 Guardsman

The Guardsman started out as one of many similar designs, the best known of which was the Seversky P-35. After Alexander de Seversky left the company named for him and formed Republic Aviation, a large number of the EP-1 version was ordered by Swedish air officials. The first batch was delivered, but those remaining from the order for 100 were taken over by the U.S. Army Air Corps as soon as sales of military aircraft to Sweden were banned in October 1940.

The EP-1s were sent to American units in the Philippines as P-35As, while almost the entire order of 50 that had been modified for use as dive bombers, were re-designated AT-12 and distributed to training fields. They were used for miscellaneous purposes, and when the war ended, all but two were broken up.

The basic concept upon which the P-35 and its progeny were designed was a sound one, as it ultimately led to the Republic P-47 Thunderbolt fighter.

Of the remaining two, one vanished and the other sat around waiting for some kind soul to take mercy on it and restore this novel craft for at least static display status. When the transcontinental Bendix Trophy Race was resumed after the war, well-known actor Buddy Rogers acquired it and had it prepared for the 1949 running of the race. Carrying #61 and NX-55811, it was flown by Vincent Perron, but got no further from the California start than Colorado before engine problems ended its very brief career.

The airplane on display is almost certainly the only one of its kind.

Specifications

Length: 27ft 8in
Wingspan: 41ft 0in
Gross weight: 8,360lb
Maximum speed: 285mph

Surviving Example

USAAC 41-17515 – Planes of Fame

Curtiss SNC-1 Falcon

What eventually became the Falcon saw the first light of day in 1935 as the Model 19, a low-powered (90hp Lambert radial engine) airplane with fixed, spatted landing gear that was meant for the private market. A few were sold to smaller air forces, but the project

was never considered a success, except that it led directly to the Curtiss-Wright Model 21, which looked like a 19 with retractable landing gear, but was a significantly different airplane.

The CW-21 Demon had a 1,000hp Wright R-1820 Cyclone radial engine which, it was claimed, gave it a rate of climb in the 5,000ft/min range and top speed close to 315mph. The prototype flew in January 1939 and soon 35 were bought by the Chinese Air Force, armed with various combinations of .30 cal. and/or .50 cal. machine guns.

There were plans to build a CW-21A with a 1,000+hp Allison V-12, but this did not materialize. An improved CW-21B, with inward retracting (in place of rearward retracting) landing gear was sold to the Dutch East Indies Air Force. It got into combat against the Japanese Ki.43 Oscar and A6M Zero, and while its very

low flying weight resulting from the omission of self-sealing fuel tanks and armor protection for the pilot made it a good dogfighter, it lacked the needed armament. Because of this and because better airplanes were in the pipeline, the U.S. military expressed no great interest

Enter the CW-22, the prototype of which flew in 1940. It shared the basic airframe with the CW-19 and CW-21, but had a smaller engine than the CW-21 – a 300hp Wright R-975 Whirlwind – it was lighter than the CW-21 and some 20mph faster than the North American SNJ/AT-6 which would replace it.

Thirty-six CW-22s were sold to the Dutch East Indies, some of which were captured by the Japanese and at least one flown. About 100 of the CW-22B export version were sold, 50 to Turkey, 25 to the Dutch and 25 to Latin American air forces.

The U.S Navy liked the CW-22N, adopting it as the SNC-1 despite its reputation for difficult landing characteristics and what turned out to be a serious weakness in the small-diameter aft fuselage. A total of 455 were delivered to the Navy, which retired most of them when the SNJ became operational.

Specifications

Length: 27ft 0in
Wingspan: 35ft 0in
Height: 10ft 11in
Wing area: 174 sq ft
Take-off weight: 3,800lb
Maximum speed: 198mph
Maximum range: 780 miles
Service ceiling: 21,800ft

CW-22N
N888U – Fantasy of Flight

SNC-1
BuAer 05194 – U.S. National Museum of Naval Aviation

Naval Aircraft Factory N3N "Yellow Peril"

The U.S. Navy had a long tradition of building its own ships, and so when there was a need for a limited number of flying boats as World War I approached, the Navy established its own factory since no private firms were interested in such a small contract. After that war, funds were in such short supply that no large orders were placed with any commercial manufacturers, and so the Naval Aircraft Factory regularly found itself filling the gap.

This continued until a second world war was becoming a distinct possibility, and the Navy saw the developing need for large numbers of trainers and scouts and even dirigibles. In 1934, the Navy's Bureau of Aeronautics (BuAer) ordered the Naval Aircraft Factory to design and build a replacement for Consolidated's NY trainer, which had been in service since 1926.

The result was the N3N, which was commonly, but never officially called the "Yellow Peril", as it, along with other Navy trainers, was to be painted that color. It was a perfectly conventional design: a two-winged, four-aileron craft with tandem open cockpits, and landing gear consisting of either wheels or a single main float and two smaller tip floats.

Power for the XN3N-1 prototype, which flew in August 1935, was a 220hp, 9-cylinder radial Wright R-790 (civil J-5) Whirlwind.

A problem with poor spin recovery was corrected by increasing the size of the rudder, but not even the extension of the motor mounts could cure its tail-heaviness. An order for 85 N3N-1s, 60 of which were to have floats, was placed in April 1936, using R-790s that had long been in Navy storage.

Sufficient improvements in flying qualities of these airplanes led to more orders, and the switch to the 235hp, 7-cylinder Wright J-6 Whirlwind 7. Continued efforts were made to solve the balance problem, with little effect. Finally in 1939 modifications eliminated most of the troublesome characteristics of the airplanes and resulted in the N3N-3. With more power, it could take off and climb much better, and the pilots' visibility was improved.

Of almost 1,000 built by the time the assembly line was closed down in early 1942, a few went to the U.S. Coast Guard for miscellaneous uses, others went to the U.S. Marine Corps as glider tugs, and the bulk went to the Navy in the primary training function for which they had been intended. Most of them had been retired by the approach of the end of the war, aside from 100 that remained in service until 1961, when they ceased to be used and the Navy thus ended its long love affair with strut-braced biplanes.

Specifications

Length: 25ft 6in
Wingspan: 34ft 0in
Height: 10ft 10in
Wing area: 305 sq ft
Empty weight: 2,090lb
Maximum speed: 126mph
Maximum range: 470 miles
Service ceiling: 15,200ft

Surviving Examples

N3N-3
BuAer 2951 – Kalamazoo Air Zoo, Michigan
BuAer 2693 and/or 3046 – U.S. National Museum of Naval Aviation
BuAer 3022 – U.S. National Air & Space Museum
BuAer 4497 – Pima Air and Space Museum

Timm N2T-1 Tutor

Young Otto Timm built his first airplane – a copy of a Curtiss pusher – in 1911. In 1922, he made history by giving Charles Lindbergh his first airplane ride. In the succeeding years he founded aircraft manufacturing companies and built several airplanes that attracted limited attention. Not until the U.S. military realized in the late

1930s that it would soon need a flood of trainers with which to teach young men to fly did he consider entering the Army Air Corps competition for a primary trainer.

Unlike the other prototypes built by his rivals, his S-160-K was built almost entirely of Timm Aeromold. This consisted of three criss-crossed layers of thin strips of spruce veneer bonded with casein glue, which was formed in a mold. The halves thus created were glued onto a conventional wooden framework. The result was a very smooth exterior for the wings and fuselage and a hint of things to come when high-tech composites became all the rage. Moreover, it used almost no aluminum, which was expected to be in short supply once the aircraft industry was working at full speed.

Unlucky for Mr Timm, the big winners of the competition were Stearman with its PT-17 biplane and Fairchild with its PT-19 monoplane. This left the Navy, which was slightly behind in its drive to expand. Once the original 160hp Kinner 5-cylinder radial engine was replaced with a 220hp Continental radial, a contract was eventually signed in 1943 after extensive testing, when 260 of the N2T-1s were ordered

When the last Navy trainer had been delivered, Timm was finished building its own-designed airplanes. Several hundred CG-4A troop-carrying gliders were built on contract, along with other farmed-out work. Otto Timm's final effort in aviation was on the patched-together airplane around which the movie "Flight of the Phoenix" was built.

After the war, a few dozen of the remaining airplanes were sold on the government surplus market for as little as $600. The saddest day in the Timm story came in September 1951, when a pilot on a cross-country flight spontaneously decided to join in an air show in Flager, Colorado, failed to complete an aerobatic maneuver and crashed into the crowd, killing 19 spectators and himself. This led to a crackdown on air shows by the CAA (now the FAA), which dogged them for several years.

Specifications

Length: 24ft 10in
Wingspan: 36ft 0in
Height: 10ft 8in
Wing area: 185 sq ft
Empty weight: 1,940lb
Maximum speed: 144mph
Maximum range: 400 miles
Service ceiling: 16,000ft
Rate of climb: 900ft/min

Surviving Examples

U.S. National Museum of Naval Aviation
BuAer 32622 – Kalamazoo Air Zoo, Michigan
c/n 281 – John Drews

Consolidated N2Y Fleet 1

It was a typical early 1930s light biplane, with quite reasonable performance for its low power. A direct descendant of the Fleet Model 1 (also called the Consolidated Model 14 Husky), it was intended as Consolidated's entry into the civil market. Before any could be built, the rights were transferred to the new Fleet Aircraft Co., formed by Consolidated President Reuben Fleet, who was its designer.

More than 300 were built in the first year of production, at which time Consolidated made Fleet a subsidiary and opened a branch plant in Canada. There, about 600 more were produced for the Royal Canadian Air Force (RCAF) in the form of the Fleet Fawn and Finch.

The U.S. Army took a close look at the machine in 1930 and ordered one prototype, 10 for service tests and just 6 "production" examples as the PT-6A, which was a Model 7, like the Fawn.

It was in U.S. Navy service that the airplane came to public attention. Six were ordered as N2Y-1 trainers after large hooks were installed above the cockpit so they could be used to attach to a "trapeze" slung beneath a dirigible, which would then become a flying aircraft carrier. The U.S. Navy's *Akron* and *Macon* were being prepared for operational use carrying several Curtiss F6C Sparrowhawk pursuit airplanes, and the N2Y's were needed for the highly specialized hooking and releasing from a huge lighter-than-air craft in full flight.

The training went well, as did the subsequent period of learning to fly the Sparrowhawks from dirigibles. The transition to operational use ended when both the *Arkon* and the *Macon* were lost in fatal crashes.

Specifications

Length: 24ft 10in
Wingspan: 36ft 0in
Height: 10ft 8in
Wing area: 185 sq ft
Empty weight: 1,940lb
Maximum speed: 144mph
Maximum range: 400 miles

Service ceiling: 16,000ft
Rate of climb: 900ft/min

Surviving Example

BuAer A-8605 – U.S. National Museum of Naval Aviation

Meyers OTW

This airplane was a de facto military type, as it was used to train military pilots under the Civilian Pilot Training Program (CPTP) and later War Training Service (WTS), but was never officially sold to the U.S. military and never received an Army or Navy designation. It is included to make the coverage of this book more complete.

Al Meyers had dreams of producing large numbers of the open-cockpit biplane he built in 1936, for it had good performance and was durable. Unfortunately, it was neither traditional, despite its fabric-covered wood wings and out-dated thin airfoil, nor modern, with its all-metal fuselage and tail. Moreover, it cost more to operate than the popular 50hp Pipers and Taylorcrafts of the day. It didn't sell.

At least it didn't until the U.S. Government set up its Civilian Pilot Training Program (CPTP) in 1939 to cope with the expected booming need for primary trainers as World War II approached. This was a university-based plan to provide ground school and up to 50 hours of flight training, and was free until the war began. Then it became the War Training Service, and required an entrant to enter the military upon graduation. Eventually more than 1,100 schools churned out more than 435,000 novice pilots before it was ended in 1944.

Specifications

Length: 22ft 6in
Wingspan: 30ft
Height: 8ft 6in
Wing area: 262 sq ft
Empty weight: 1,207lb
Maximum speed: 120mph
Maximum range: 275 miles
Service ceiling: 17,500ft
Rate of climb: 1,200ft/min

Surviving Examples

c/n 001, NC-15784 (prototype) – Combat Air Museum, Topeka, Kansas
c/n 102, NC-34357 (last built) – EAA Museum

For financial reasons, most schools preferred low-powered airplanes like the Piper J-3 Cub and Aeronca Defender, which became the L-4 and L-3 liaison planes, respectively. Then an opening appeared for the Meyers, by now known as the OTW, standing for "Out to Win". Some schools added a course in aerobatics to their basic curriculum, and with its two large wings and open cockpits, the OTW fit the bill.

One hundred of the spindly-looking biplanes were produced for the civilian schools, where they performed well. After the war, many were grabbed up by sportsmen, and operators of crop dusting firms. Today, an OTW is among the more treasured of the economical-to-operate classics.

Great Britain

Miles M.14 Magister/Hawk Trainer III

Until the middle of the 1930s it was acceptable to the Royal Air Force to start its pilot trainees out in strut-and-wire-braced biplanes, since many of them would be flying airplanes of that design in active squadrons. Starting with the Avro 504 and continuing through the deHavilland Tiger Moth, they had been more than sufficient, as the ultimate goal was to fly Gloster Gladiators and Hawker Furys. But in the mid-1930s aircraft manufacturers and their customers in the RAF began to think seriously in terms of cantilever low-wing monoplanes such as the Hawker Hurricane and Supermarine Spitfire.

It was then obvious that the same path had to be taken with the trainers which would prepare novices for the more modern fighters. The first to appear was the Magister, a direct descendant of the private sporting Hawk Major and Hawk Trainer. It became not merely the RAF's first monoplane training airplane, but also the first of its type to be approved for aerobatic instruction, once its reticence in recovering from spins was corrected.

The prototype Magister flew in March 1937, built up from a basically spruce frame, covered with plywood. Changes included larger cockpits and more instruments. After tests revealed some difficulty in recovering from spins, the rudder was enlarged and strakes (low-profile vertical fins) were added to the rudder; it was put in production in October 1937 as the M.14A Magister I.

Magister Is and IIs were powered by the 130hp deHavilland Gipsy Major I, while the III used the 135hp Blackburn Cirrus II, both being four-cylinder, air-cooled, inline engines.

By the start of the war, more than 700 Magisters were in RAF service, having been delivered to Elementary Flying Training Schools, along with others that had been impressed from their civilian owners. In total, some 1,300 were built from 1937 through 1941, including 100 on license in Turkey. They operated with the RAF, British Army and Royal Navy. After the war, many of those surviving the rigors of student use were snapped up for private use and were called the Hawk Trainer III.

Specifications

Length: 24ft 7in
Wingspan: 33ft 10in
Height: 9ft 1in
Wing area: 176 sq ft
Empty weight: 1,260lb
Maximum speed: 132mph
Maximum range: 380 miles
Service ceiling: 18,000ft
Rate of climb: 850ft/min

Surviving Examples

RAF BB661 – Imperial War Museum, Duxford,
RAF P.6382 – Shuttleworth Collection, Old Warden Aerodrome

de Havilland dH.82A Tiger Moth

The sporty Tiger Moth evokes feelings of nostalgia in Great Britain much like the Piper J-3 Cub in the U.S.A. So many wartime and peacetime pilots received their introduction to the pleasures and

primary trainer to replace the Avro 504, which it had been using for the purpose since World War I. Deliveries began in early 1932, and more than 1,000 were serving with RAF Elementary and Reserve Flying Training Schools when the war started.

The original Mk.I used a 120hp deHavilland Gipsy III engine, replaced for the Mk.II by the 130hp Gipsy Major. All had wooden structures, with a combination of plywood and fabric covering. Few significant changes were made during the production run which ended in 1944.

A total of 8,868 Tiger Moths were built, with 4,200 made during the war, most of them on contract by the Morris Motor Co. Almost 3,000 more were built by deHavilland Canada as the DH.82C with strengthened landing gear and a closed canopy to keep some of the bitter Canadian winter weather at bay. That company also delivered 200 trainers to the USAAF as the PT-24.

Ex-RAF Tiger Moths were a best-seller among types declared surplus after the war, quickly equipping flying schools and flying clubs and individual owners with an airplane that had no equal for economical purchase price and running costs. Scores of small airfields around Britain have at least one of the classic biplanes parked on the ramp or in a hangar.

challenges of flying through them that these airplanes are now valued collectors' items, several decades later.

De Havilland gave birth to the British light airplane, when its dH.60 Gipsy Moth first left the ground in 1925. Unlike contemporary private airplanes, it offered a combination of good flying qualities, low initial and operating costs and folding wings for more convenient hangarage.

Its successor, the Tiger Moth, arrived in 1931 with a more powerful 120hp Gipsy II mounted inverted for better ground clearance. In addition, the upper wing was swept back for easier entry into the front and rear cockpits, along with a beefed-up structure and small fold-down doors on either side of the cockpit.

It was an instant hit with small flying schools, and was an obvious choice when, in 1931, the RAF needed a more modern

Specifications

Length: 23ft 11in
Wingspan: 29ft 4in
Height: 8ft 9in
Wing area: 239 sq ft
Empty weight: 1,115lb
Maximum speed: 109mph
Maximum range: 300 miles

Service ceiling: 13,600ft
Rate of climb: 670ft/min

Some Surviving Examples

dH.82A
RAF DE998 – Imperial War Museum, Duxford,
RAF T6818 – Shuttleworth Collection, Old Warden Aerodrome
RAF – Museum of Flight, East Fortune, Scotland
The Fighter Factory

Mk.II
RAF T6296 – RAF Museum, Hendon

dH.82C Menasco Moth
RCAF 4861 – Canadian Air & Space Museum, Ottawa

Avro Anson

The Anson began its military career in the maritime reconnaissance role, keeping an aerial eye on many hundreds of miles of British coastline for the recently formed Coastal Command. It soon became obsolete and was replaced by more modern Lockheed Hudsons and Armstrong Whitworth Whitleys. Quickly turned into a multi-purpose trainer, it was eventually produced in quantities exceeded only by the Vickers Wellington medium bomber among all British types of aircraft.

The Anson was developed from a six-seat airliner, and was flown in prototype military form in March 1935. It became the first British military airplane to have retractable landing gear, though the need to turn a hand crank 140 rotations could hardly heave endeared it to those who were to fly it, even though it provided a 30mph speed increase over the unfaired fixed landing gear.

By the time the war began in September 1939, the RAF had equipped 16 Bomber Command and 10 Coastal Command squadrons with Anson Mk.Is. They had already become obsolete, at least partly due to their basically wood construction, and were retired as quickly as Hudsons and Whitleys could replace them. The end of the Anson appeared imminent.

Enter Training Command, which was in serious need of a twin-engined airplane with which to train not only pilots but navigators, radio operators, bombardiers and gunners. A fly-off against a military version of the deHavilland 89 Dragon Rapide biplane was decided in favor of the Anson, which went into large-scale production.

The military Anson differed from the civil Type 652 airliner in its manually-operated top turret and the installation of larger square cabin windows, along with an up-rated version of its Armstrong

Siddeley Cheetah radial engines. Just before the war, an order was placed for 1,500 airplanes equipped with wing flaps.

The rapidly prepared RAF flying schools in Canada, safe from German bombers, were assigned Anson Mk.IIIs with American Jacobs engines and Mk.IVs with Wright engines. Mks.X through XII were modified for use as cargo transports and flying ambulances, while later versions had roomier fuselages, and versions starting with the Mk.XII had metal wings.

Production continued until 1952, well after the end of the war. By then, 11,020 had been built. The RAF retired its last in 1968, while the air force of Afghanistan operated a few Ansons as late as 1972, resulting in a 36-year term of military service for an airplane almost retired in its early years.

Specifications

Length: 42ft 3in
Wingspan: 56ft 6in
Height: 13ft 1in
Wing area: 463 sq ft
Empty weight: 6,610lb
Maximum speed: 188mph
Maximum range: 790 miles
Service ceiling: 19,000ft
Rate of climb: 750ft/min

Surviving Examples

Mk.1
RAF T6296 – Royal Air Force Museum, Hendon
RAF N4877– Imperial War Museum, Duxford

Mk.II
British Columbia Aviation Museum, Canada
Aerospace Museum of Calgary, Canada

Mk.V
RCAF 12518 – Canadian National Museum

C.19
RAF TX213 – North East Air Museum
RAF TX214 – Royal Air Force Museum, Cosford
RAF TX226 – Imperial War Museum, Duxford
RAF VL348 – Newark Air Museum

Airspeed Oxford I

The Oxford resembled the Anson in both appearance and purpose, both being twin-engined monoplane trainers with retractable landing gear. While the Anson was a combat airplane converted to the training role, the Oxford was meant as a trainer from the start.

Forerunner of the Oxford was the eight-passenger Envoy domestic airliner, which, with minor changes, became a versatile advanced trainer when it entered RAF service in 1938 and Royal Navy service in 1939. Like the Anson, it used a pair of 375hp air-cooled Armstrong Siddeley Cheetah, having seven cylinders and 835 cubic inches piston displacement. The prototype flew in June 1937 and by the following November the type was in service at the Central Flying School.

When World War II broke out, the Oxford went into large-scale production alongside the slightly older Anson for the Empire Air Training Scheme, which involved not only Great Britain but the entire British Commonwealth, meaning in particular Canada,

Australia, New Zealand and various African and Middle Eastern countries' air forces. In some of the latter nations, Oxfords were converted in the field to serve as light bombers.

The internal arrangements could be easily converted from one use to another: navigator, radio operator, bombardier and aerial photography training. Mk.I Oxfords had a hand-operated turret with a single .30 cal. machine gun mounted atop the fuselage.

More than 8,700 Oxfords were built and played a major role in training more than 135,000 pilots and aircrew.

Specifications

Length: 34ft 6in
Wingspan: 53ft 4in
Height: 11ft 1in
Wing area: 348 sq ft
Empty weight: 5,320lb
Maximum speed: 192mph
Service ceiling: 23,500ft
Rate of climb: 1,340ft/min

Surviving Examples

Mk.I
RAF MP425 – RAF Museum, Hendon,
RAF V3388 – Imperial War Museum, Duxford
BAF 016 – Belgian Aviation Museum, Brussels

Percival Proctor

Edgar Percival formed his company in 1932, and within a few years had established a reputation for fast, visually appealing airplanes which so exceeded the performance of contemporary rivals that they were used to set dozens of long-distance speed records and win numerous races. His original Gull led to the slightly larger Vega Gull and then the sleek Mew Gull.

When the British Air Ministry needed a new communications/utility airplane in 1938, Percival adapted his Vega Gull to the specific requirements of the military services, thus creating the Proctor, powered by a 210hp single deHavilland Gipsy Queen II. The prototype, with an entirely wooden structure and fabric covering, flew in October 1939. Such was the state of affairs at the time, the Proctor was briefly considered as a light bomber in view of the strong possibility of a German invasion embarking from occupied France.

The Proctor Mk.I was a three-seat airplane with dual controls, of which 247 were built for the RAF and used for a wide variety of purposes. Next came the single-control Proctor Mk.II, identical except for specialized equipment needed to train radio operators and of which 50 were produced.

The Proctor Mk.III was also a radio trainer, and 437 (all but the prototype) were built under license by F. Hills & Sons. The final military version – the Proctor Mk.IV – had a widened fuselage to seat an additional passenger and additional radio equipment. Many of these were then converted to utility use with dual flight controls. Production amounted to 250, bringing the grand total to just under 1,000.

Following the end of the war, many Mks. I, II and III were sold as surplus and found their way back into personal and sport flying. The Mk.IV remained in service as late as 1955. The final version was the Proctor C. Mk.V, of which some 150 were built, a few for the RAF.

Specifications

Length: 28ft 2in
Wingspan: 39ft 6in
Height: 7ft 3in
Wing area: 202 sq ft
Empty weight: 2,375lb
Maximum speed: 160mph
Maximum range: 500 miles
Service ceiling: 14,000ft
Rate of climb: 700ft/min

Surviving Examples

Proctor III
AF LZ766 – Imperial War Museum, Duxford,
RAF NP191 – Musee Royal de l'Armee, Brussels
RAF Z7197 – RAF Museum, Hendon

Proctor IV
RAF RM221 (G-ANXR) – Biggin Hill
RAF NP294 – Lincolnshire Aviation Heritage Centre

Proctor V
m/s AE-84 – Musee Royal de l'Armee, Brussels

General Aircraft Cygnet

When France fell in 1940, many Douglas A-20 light bombers (from French orders for almost 1,000) found their way to Britain, where their outstanding performance was tempered by a few problem areas. One of these was the A-20s tricycle landing gear, then a novelty. In order to acclimatize pilots to the different behavior on the ground, the RAF acquired five little Cygnets from their private owners.

The Cygnet dated back to 1936 when it was the first British-built light plane with stressed skin construction. The prototype flew in May 1937 with a traditional tail wheel. It and subsequent civil Cygnets used a 150hp 4-cylinder, inline Blackburn Cirrus Major II engine.

The production version, called the Cygnet II, had a nose wheel and would undoubtedly have sold well, but only 10 had been built when the war ended production. In addition to the five mentioned before, two more were impressed by the government for utility/liaison use.

Avro Tutor

It wasn't easy to replace the Avro 504 as the RAF's main primary trainer. It had been in service since 1913, and had served as a bomber and scout during World War I. As evidence of its durability, the final 504N version remained in production until 1933. Eventually, despite the affection which so many pilots felt for it, the 504 had to be replaced.

Even then, the RAF seemed of two minds about retiring one of its classic airplanes. The first replacements were the Avro Trainer and the Hawker Tomtit, both ordered in small numbers in 1930. Eventually an improvement of the Trainer, called the Tutor, replaced the last of the old 504s. After just 21 Trainers were built, production accelerated and 381 Tutors and 15 Avro Sea Tutors (on floats) were delivered to the RAF.

The Trainer had a basic structure of steel tubing covered with fabric, and was powered by a 155hp Armstrong Siddeley Mongoose radial engine.

Specifications

Length: 23ft 3in
Wingspan: 34ft 6in
Height: 7ft 0in
Wing area: 179 sq ft
Empty weight: 1,475lb
Maximum speed: 135mph
Maximum range: 445 miles
Service ceiling: 14,000ft
Rate of climb: 800ft/min

Surviving Example

RAF MP425 or ES915 – Museum of Flight, East Fortune, Scotland

The Tutor was aerodynamically cleaner and more powerful than its predecessor, and, fitted with a 180hp Armstrong Siddeley Lynx IV radial engine, reduced the performance gap between trainers and operational airplanes.

As war approached, the need for a large quantity of trainers forced a reevaluation of the types becoming available. The winner was the deHavilland Tiger Moth Mk.II, whose consumption of fuel and oil was barely half that of the Avro, with the result that while the latter was built by the hundreds, the Tiger Moth was built by the thousands.

When the war began, over half the production run of Tutors and Sea Tutors were still operational, a testament to the type's durability. They gradually were transferred to utility uses, and when the war ended, hardly any were left for the civil market.

Specifications

Length: 26ft 5in
Wingspan: 34ft 0in
Height: 9ft 7in
Wing area: 301 sq ft
Empty weight: 1,845lb
Maximum speed: 120mph
Maximum range: 250 miles
Service ceiling: 16,000ft
Rate of climb: 910ft/min

Surviving Example

K3241 – Old Warden Aerodrome

Australia

CAC Wackett

The manufacture of civil and military airplanes in large numbers was not a familiar matter to Australians. Until the approach of World War II, they had been able to buy the limited numbers of airplanes they needed from other countries. But as war drew closer, it became obvious that the main sources – Great Britain and the U.S.A. – would need all the airplanes they could build for their own purposes.

In 1938, the Royal Australian Air Force decided it required an *ab initio* (primary) trainer. This resulted in the first locally designed airplane to come from the Commonwealth Aircraft Corp. of Australia. The Wackett, a tandem two-seater, was a low-wing monoplane with wings and tail built of wood, and a steel tube fuselage with extensive fabric covering. The prototype, which made its first flight in late 1939, had a four-cylinder deHavilland Gipsy Major engine, which proved to be underpowered. It was replaced by a six-cylinder Gipsy, which was more powerful but also much heavier. Finally, an American Warner Scarab radial engine provided the needed power at the desired weight.

In 1940, when the supply of foreign airplanes and engines could no longer be counted on, the RAAF ordered production of 200 Wacketts, and the first indigenous example flew in February 1941. Acquisition of Hamilton Standard propellers proved a problem, and a large number of otherwise complete airplanes accumulated at the factory, where they were conveniently located for improvements to be incorporated before delivery.

Additional delays were caused by the need to build Boomerang fighters, once war had broken out in the Pacific in December 1941. At last, Wacketts were rolling off the assembly line and by April,

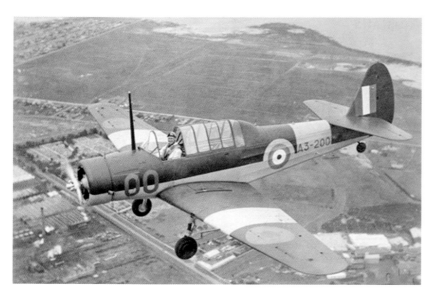

Empty weight: 1,910lb
Maximum speed: 115mph
Maximum range: 425 miles

Surviving Examples

RAAF A3-22 – Australian National Aviation Museum, Moorabbin
RAAF A3-139 – Central Australian Aviation Museum
Post-war KS-3 Cropmaster VH-AJH – Queensland Air Museum

CAC Wirraway

Once the Royal Australian Air Force was on the way to a locally manufactured primary trainer, it obviously needed an advanced trainer if its new pilots were to become prepared to fly combat airplanes. A visit to American aircraft factories convinced Lawrence Wackett, of the Commonwealth Aircraft Co., that North American Aviation was on the right track to what would soon be the highly successful AT-6 Texan/Harvard.

Arrangements were made to import examples of NAA's fixed landing gear BT-9 and retractable BC-1. Both arrived in Australia in the late summer of 1937, with flight tests pointing toward the BC-1 which became the RAAF's CA-1, once some modifications were completed. Without a variety of new military airplanes to choose among, it was determined that with the addition of a second .30 cal. machine gun and some structural beefing-up, the newly-named Wirraway (an aboriginal word meaning "challenge") could also be used for ground support and even dive bombing.

After 40 CA-1s were built, a contract was signed for 60 CA-3s, which differed little from the CA-1. Additional contracts were for basically similar CA-5s (32 examples), followed by 100 CA-

1942, all 200 had been delivered to the RAAF. They were used at many training fields around Australia.

After some 75 were seriously damaged or destroyed on training flights by the end of the war, the remainder were sold as surplus to military needs. Thirty were sold to the Indonesians and more went onto the Australian civil register for personal use. Later, several were converted into agricultural airplanes as Cropmasters.

Specifications

Length: 26ft 0in
Wingspan: 37ft 0in
Height: 9ft 10in

from a large force of Japanese bombers and their fighter cover. No combination of skill and courage could compensate for the terrible odds, and only two of the Wirraways returned without having suffered serious damage.

Efforts to support ground forces with these converted trainers continued until supplies of purpose-built Boomerang fighters and American Curtiss P-40s could be found. A few years after the war, the Royal Australian Navy formed its own flying units and made use of Wirraway trainers until the era of the jet began in the late 1950s.

Sales of military surplus Wirraways were brisk, though they resisted conversion to agricultural uses. Private owners continue to fly them and prolong the unusual history of one of their country's first aircraft manufacturing efforts.

Specifications

Length: 27ft 10in
Wingspan: 43ft 0in
Height: 8ft 9in
Wing area: 256 sq ft
Empty weight: 3,990lb
Maximum speed: 220mph
Maximum range: 720 miles
Service ceiling: 23,000ft
Rate of climb: 1,950ft/min

Surviving Examples

RAAF A20-10 – Australian National Aviation Museum, Moorabbin
Civil VH-MFW – Caboolture Warplane Museum

7s, 200 CA-8s and 188 CA-9s. Not until it was decided to order 135 CA-16s were any significant changes made, including "dive bomber wings" which could carry a greater bomb load, and dive brakes. All models of the Wirraway, as well as its predecessors and thousands of AT-6s, were powered by the 600hp Pratt & Whitney R-1350 Wasp radial, air-cooled engine.

All through the war the Wirraway shouldered the advanced training load, enabling many hundreds of pilots from not only Australia but also New Zealand to proceed to bigger and better things. The last Wirraway trainer was produced in 1946 and remained in service until 1959.

With vast areas to be patrolled, it was inevitable that Wirraways were pressed into uses for which they were simply not suited. Armed with but two small machine guns each, a group of eight set out to protect Rabaul, in what is now Papua New Guinea,

Canada

Fleet Finch II

It was like a deHavilland Tiger Moth that had been adapted to Canada's unique conditions. It had a closed canopy to prevent the instructor (and perhaps even the student pilot) from freezing solid during the hard winters, and balloon tires for the inevitable forced landings in farmers' fields. The American-built engine was an added attraction.

The Finch dates back to 1930 and the slow production and sale of Fleet 10 primary trainers for civilian use. The RCAF took notice of the latest version, called the Fleet 16, in 1938. Official tests resulted in few changes before production began in 1939 of a quite conventional airplane having a steel tube fuselage structure and the rest built of wood covered with either plywood or fabric.

The military prototype was powered by a 175hp, 7-cylinder Warner Super Scarab radial engine, which was replaced with a 160hp five-cylinder Kinner radial for the two production models: the 16R, of which 27 were built for the RCAF; and the Model 16B, powered by an uprated Kinner, and which was built in a quantity of 400. In addition, 15 were delivered to the Portuguese Navy with 160hp Kinner engines.

The Finch served the Canadian forces until late 1944, when both it and the deHavilland Tiger Moth were replaced by the more modern Fairchild PT-26 Cornell. The last Finch was officially retired in 1947.

Specifications

Length: 21ft 8in
Wingspan: 28ft 0in
Height: 7ft 9in
Wing area: 194 sq ft
Empty weight: 1,220lb
Maximum speed: 104mph
Maximum range: 300 miles
Service ceiling: 10,500ft
Rate of climb: 435ft/min

Surviving Examples

RCAF 4510 – Canadian National Aviation Museum, Ottawa
RCAF 4725 – British Columbia Aviation Museum

France

Morane Saulnier M.S.230

The standard French Air Force primary trainer of the 1930s descended from a long line of military airplanes, dating back to the pre-World War I period. Unlike the usual biplane trainers, it was a parasol-wing design, permitting a much better view of the ground during take offs, landings and frantic searches for emergency landing fields.

The prototype was the M.S.229, built in 1929 with a Hispano-Suiza V-8, and went into production the next year with a 230hp Salmson 9-cylinder radial engine. Construction was composed of a steel tubing framework covered with fabric. More than 1,000 were built, with many going to flying clubs and to private owners. Exports included 25 to Greece, 10 to Rumania and even a few to Nazi Germany.

The M.S. 231 through M.S. 237 were basically similar to the 230, with variations in engines up to 230hp, the 232 being powered by a Clerget diesel. The M.S. 237MH was on floats, while a specially modified M.S. 234 was flown in aerobatic contests by Michel Detroyat. Many remain in France and elsewhere and are used for sport and display flying.

Specifications

Length: 22ft 10in
Wingspan: 35ft 1in
Height: 9ft 2in
Wing area: 212 sq ft
Empty weight: 1,830lb
Maximum speed: 127mph

Maximum range: 360 miles
Service ceiling: 16,400ft

Surviving Examples

c/n 1038 – Brussels Air Museum
c/n 1048 – Musee de l'Air
c/n 1077 – Prague-Kbely Museum

Union of Soviet Socialist Republics

Polikarpov Po-2

Just because it was originally called the U-2 doesn't mean it was a high-altitude spy plane. In this case, it was (and still is) a large, angular biplane with long wings and a small engine that produces a cruising speed under 80mph. Despite what should be serious drawbacks, more of them were built than almost any other type

of World War II airplane. The exact, or even approximate number built is not known, thanks to the poor record keeping of the U.S.S.R. Expert estimates range from just under 30,000 to slightly over 40,000.

The first primary trainer acquired by the Red Air Force following the 1918 war was the Avro 504, which it called the U-1. The first prototype of the follow-on U-2 didn't fly until June 1927, on the limited power of a 100hp 5-cylinder Shevetsov radial engine. A year and a half later, pre-production airplanes were under test in realistic military conditions, and it went into production in 1929 with a future no one could possibly have imagined.

Right from the start, its versatility was taken advantage of, with an agricultural version built alongside the trainer, which, in turn,

was soon in use as a specialized transport and a liaison airplane carrying supplies to groups of partisans located behind the front lines separating the Soviet and German armies.

As improbable as it may seem for such slow airplanes, they went into use as night bombers, carrying very small loads of bombs which they dropped while gliding quietly at very low altitude over sleeping German troops. The technique was resurrected during the Korean War by North Korean pilots who became a major sleep-depriving nuisance to the UN forces. In both cases, the great difference in speed in comparison with defending fighters made interception particularly difficult.

As the airplane progressed through dozens of wartime and then post-war versions and uses, power increased from the initially standard 100hp M-11 radial to a 150hp improvement, and while take-off and climb performance were raised, level speed showed little increase. Additional uses included an ambulance airplane, a floatplane, a two-passenger civil transport, and a propaganda version fitted with a large loud speaker.

In 1944, upon the death of designer Nikolai Polikarpov, the designation was changed from the functional to the honorific Po-2, which was applied retroactively to many older versions of the amazingly versatile open-cockpit biplane.

Specifications (U-2)

Length: 26ft 10in
Wingspan: 37ft 5in
Height: 10ft 2in
Wing area: 357 sq ft
Empty weight: 2,375lb
Maximum speed: 94mph
Maximum range: 390 miles
Service ceiling: 9,850ft
Rate of climb: 545ft/min

Surviving Examples

Russian Air Force Museum, Monino
The Fighter Factory
U.S.S.R. 641543 – Flying Heritage Collection
Prague-Kbely Air Museum, Czech Republic

Yakovlev UT-2

As the speed of Soviet fighters and bombers increased thanks to improved aerodynamics and bigger engines, the need for a trainer of higher performance than the ponderous U-2/Po-2 became inescapable. A 1935 design competition for an airplane to be used strictly for training was won by Yakovlev's AIR-10, which became the Red Air Force's principal trainer.

In 1938 the designation which had recognized designer A.I. Rykov, who had been among the tens of thousands murdered in Josef Stalin's mass purge of military and industrial leaders, was changed briefly to Ya-20 and then to UT-2.

In contrast to the Polikarpov Po-2, the new UT-2 was not as easy for brand new student pilots to fly, having an especially troublesome tendency to enter a spin. Major changes were made to the design, including new wings and an enlarged vertical fin, which improved flying characteristics. The new version – UT-2M – went into large-scale production in 1941 with a 125hp M-11D radial engine.

Despite additional improvements, some introduced in the field, the UT-2 remained a somewhat difficult airplane to fly. Nevertheless, more than 7,000 were built and credited with enabling more than 100,000 men and women to learn to fly. They remained in service until the 1950s when they were replaced by the Yak-18 primary trainer and the Yak-11 advanced trainer. Both were later modified into highly effective aerobatic mounts which enabled Soviet pilots to win numerous medals in international competition.

Specifications

Length: 23ft 6in
Wingspan: 33ft 6in

Height: 9ft 10in
Wing area: 184 sq ft
Empty weight: 1,385lb
Maximum speed: 131mph
Maximum range: 700 miles
Service ceiling: 16,400ft
Rate of climb: 950ft/min.

Surviving Example

Monino

Poland

PWS-26

From its origins as the best all-around trainer of the pre-war Polish Air Force, to its brief service as a utility airplane during the German blitzkrieg of September 1939, the PWS-26 was the epitome of an air arm lacking first-line equipment and yet fighting on.

It was the winner of a contract to replace all other Polish trainers of the period, thanks to its sturdy structure and mild flying characteristics. While quite similar to its predecessors, it was strong enough to permit being used for training dive bomber pilots.

The prototype first flew in 1935, production began in 1936 and more than 300 had been delivered to military training units by the start of hostilities. While in use as liaison airplanes for the Polish Army, several were lost to German fighters, while most others

were destroyed on the ground either by the Germans or as the defeat of Poland came closer, by the Poles to prevent them from being captured.

Almost 50 fell into German hands, with most of the remainder being transferred by the Poles to the Latvians and Rumanians. The Germans then captured most of those in Latvia and joined the few already with Rumanian forces. About a dozen were soon taken over by the invading Soviet Army and used for miscellaneous testing.

One PWS-26 is alleged to have downed a Messerschmitt Bf 109 when the Polish pilot tricked the German pilot into an ever-lower chase which is said to have ended when the German flew into the ground while trying to out-maneuver the slower but more agile trainer.

Specifications

Length: 23ft 1in
Wingspan: 29ft 6in
Height: 9ft 5in
Wing area: 269 sq ft
Empty weight: 1,950lb
Maximum speed: 125mph
Maximum range: 285 miles
Service ceiling: 13,780ft

Sole Surviving Example

Polish Air Force 81-123. Civil SP-AJB (ex-Luftwaffe VG+AS) – Polish Aviation Museum, Kracow

Germany

Bücker Bu.131 Jungmann

The manufacture of airplanes for military purposes was forbidden to Germany by the Treaty of Versailles, which ended World War I and made a sequel inevitable. When Germany decided to proceed with such production in secret, one of its first needs was for a piston-engined primary trainer for the many new pilots who had been trained to fly "sporting" gliders in Hitler Youth Glider Clubs, which were legal and widely known to be preparing pilots for the soon-to-be-revealed Luftwaffe.

Carl Bücker, who had emigrated from Germany to Sweden after the first war and become managing director of SAAB, returned

home along with one of SAAB's designers, Anders Anderson. Together, they founded Bücker Aircraft Co. in 1932, the year Hitler took control of Germany. Their first airplane was the Bu.131, a nimble trainer with good aerobatic capability.

While the new Jungmann was little larger than a modern Pitts Special aerobatic biplane, its performance was limited by the mere 80hp of its Hirth4-cylinder, air-cooled HM60R engine. By 1936 the Bu.131B was being turned out with a 105hp Hirth 504 engines. Construction was conventional, with a steel tubing fuselage covered with fabric except for the sheet aluminum engine compartment, and wings of wood structure and fabric covering.

Quantities of the Bu.131A were supplied to the German sport flying organization, a cover for military training. But by 1936, all pretense of obeying the Treaty of Versailles was dropped, and the Bu.131B became the main vehicle for the Luftwaffe primary training program. The swastika was soon being seen at flying fields and even public events.

The Jungmann was simple, rugged, easy to fly and cheap to build in the quantities to be needed for a major war. As expected, other countries were interested in what was obviously an excellent airplane, and production licenses were soon sold to Switzerland, Czechoslovakia, Japan, and others, including Yugoslavia, which built 400. The Czechs, in fact, built most of the Jungmanns used by Germany. The Japanese built no fewer than 1,037 as the Ki.86 for its Army, and 339 for its Navy as the Kyushu K9W.

The end of the war was not the end of Jungmann production, as the Spanish firm CASA continued to build them until the 1960s, and the Czechs built some 250 after the war as the Aero C-104. Of several thousand built (the exact number is not known) as many as 150 have survived to train and entertain.

Specifications (Bu-131B)

Length: 21ft 8in
Wingspan: 24ft 3in
Height: 7ft 6in
Wing area: 145 sq ft
Empty weight: 840lb
Maximum speed: 115mph
Maximum range: 390 miles
Service ceiling: 13,300ft
Rate of climb: 680ft/min

Surviving Examples

Bu-131B
A-43, D-EBAD – Deutsches Technik Museum
A-45, I-CERM – Caproni Museum, Trento
A-65, N131BU – Fantasy of Flight

CASA 1131E
Deutsches Museum, Munich

Bücker Bu.133 Jungmeister

As first a civilian trainer and then for the Luftwaffe, the Bu-133 achieved much greater fame as an air show and competition aerobatic airplane. Its career began with a first flight in 1935 and continued though World War II and well into the 1960s in both world-class and national meets.

It was a slightly smaller version of the highly successful Bu-131 primary trainer, differing mainly in having greater power, starting with a 140hp Hirth HM506 radial engine, then a 160hp Siemens-Bramo SH 14. In later years, competition pilots used engines as large as the 180–200hp Lycoming horizontally-opposed 4-cylinder O-360. The basically sturdy main structure easily accepted the increases in power.

In view of its outstanding performance in air shows, Hitler saw it as an excellent propaganda vehicle that could demonstrate National Socialism's alleged superiority in yet another field. Soon Jungmeisters were being flown to victory in prestigious competitions throughout Europe, though doubts have been raised about the propriety of the judging in some cases. Nevertheless, it was a first-rate airplane, and became a major Luftwaffe trainer.

Local interest led to production licenses to Dornier, which built 50 Jungmeisters in Switzerland, and to CASA which built 50 as the I-133 with Hirth engines in Spain; these remained in Air Force service until 1964. Negotiations to build them in Poland and the U.S.S.R. fell victim to the beginning of hostilities in 1939.

After the war the surviving Jungmeisters were in great demand, as nothing had been built that surpassed their performance. An attempt to put the airplane back into production failed, as they would have been too expensive for most potential customers. Still, the air show demonstrations in America by the likes of "Bevo" Howard whet pilots' appetites for an airplane that could snap-roll faster and climb higher.

Not until the advent of the Pitts Special S-1S, with 180 or more horsepower, was it possible to advance the sport of aerobatics from its late-1930s peak. Even today, it is possible to purchase construction drawings with which to build your own Jungmeister.

Specifications

Length: 19ft 8in
Wingspan: 21ft 8in
Height: 7ft 3in
Wing area: 129 sq ft
Empty weight: 935lb
Maximum speed: 137mph
Maximum range: 310 miles
Service ceiling: 14,765ft
Rate of climb: 1,170ft/min

Surviving Examples

Bu.133B
c/n 42, YR-PAX – U.S. National Air & Space Museum

Bu.133C
c/n 1009, E.7-14 – Museo del Aire, Madrid

Bucker Bu.181 Bestmann

In common with most other major air forces in the immediate pre-war period, Nazi Germany's Luftwaffe saw the need to proceed from classic biplane trainers to higher performance monoplanes, in keeping with the progression from biplane to monoplane fighters. The Bucker Bu.131 and 133 had performed well in training future combat pilots, but were increasingly seen as out of date.

The Bucker works had flown the prototype of its Bu.181 Bestmann trainer in February 1939 and had then seen it adopted as the standard primary trainer, with production starting in late 1940. It was a side-by-side two-seater powered by a four-cylinder inline 105hp Hirth 504A engine, and conventionally built with a steel tube forward fuselage framework and wooden shells for the aft fuselage, wings and tail. Modern equipment included split wing flaps.

Manufacturing was begun by the Bucker factory, which then licensed production to Fokker in the Netherlands, which eventually built more than 700. In addition, 125 were built on license in neutral Sweden as the Sk.25. Just before the war ended, production of the Bucker Bu.181D was begun in Czechoslovakia's Zlin factory, which continued to build them as the C.6 and C.106 for the Czech Air Force, and as the Zlin Z.281 and Z.381 sport airplanes. Almost 800 were built.

In the 1950s, Heliopolis, of Greece, was licensed by the Czechs to built 300 or more as the Gomhouria and many were sold to several Arab air forces for training use.

Specifications

Length: 25ft 8in
Wingspan: 34ft 9in
Height: 6ft 8in
Wing area: 145 sq ft
Empty weight: 1,060lb
Maximum speed: 135mph
Maximum range: 500 miles
Service ceiling: 16,400ft
Rate of climb: 620ft/min

Surviving Examples

Musee de l'Air
Fantasy of Flight

Klemm Kl.35

It had the unmistakable look of a pre-World War II sport plane: tandem open cockpits, spindly, non-retractable landing gear, graceful, internally braced inverted-gull wings. It was a direct successor to the Klemm 25 of the mid-1920s. The first one flew in February 1935, was introduced to the sporting aviation public in the following October, and was soon in production.

Supposedly a sport airplane, this one was developed under the watchful eye of the German Air Ministry, which was deeply involved in clandestine plans for rapid expansion of the Luftwaffe. Quantity manufacture of the Kl.35D began in 1938 as a primary trainer for the now openly admitted German Air Force.

The Model 35D was powered by a 105hp, 4-cylinder, inline, air-cooled Hirth HM504 engine which turned a fixed-pitch, two-bladed wooden propeller. It replaced the original's 80hp Hirth. Construction was mainly of wood, with a steel tube fuselage. Total production figures are not known, though some authorities claim as many as

many as 3,000 were built, mainly by Klemm, but also 365 by Fieseler in Germany and 75 in Sweden.

It has been estimated that, along with hundreds of sport model Klemm 35s, around 2,300 went to the Luftwaffe to be used in teaching novices the basics of piloting. Experimental versions included one with tricycle landing gear and another with floats for operations from lakes and rivers.

As the design was a good one for private sport flying, they continue to be used for that purpose in Europe, along with a few examples of this increasingly valuable classic airplane in the U.S.A.

Specifications

Length: 24ft 7in
Wingspan: 34ft 1in
Height: 6ft 9in
Wing area: 164 sq ft
Empty weight: 1,015lb
Maximum speed: 132mph
Maximum range: 415 miles
Service ceiling: 14,270ft

Surviving Examples

Kl.35
s/n 2827 – Pima Air and Space Museum
Hannover Air Museum

Kl.35D
Fv5028 – Technik Museum, Berlin
Fv5081 – Flygvapnet Museum, Sweden

Focke Wulf FW.44J Steiglitz

The lack of large airplane factories that could churn out hundreds or even dozens a month forced the German Air Ministry to contract with several different companies to design and build trainers as the second step (the first had been innocent-appearing gliders) leading to the establishment of the strongest offensive air arm in Europe. Along with Bucker and Klemm with their primary and advanced trainers, they chose to go with Focke Wulf, which had yet to build much more than prototypes.

The maker of the FW-44 biplane was soon established as a producer of military airplanes. But the FW-44 was not a success until problems with the structural stability and flight characteristics of the prototype, which first flew in 1932, had been ironed out by

new designer and test pilot Kurt Tank, who would go on to fame for his FW-190 fighter.

The pre-production model's 150hp Siemens Sh14a, an uncowled radial engine, was replaced in the FW-44B by a 110hp, 4-cylinder, 386 cu. in., inverted inline Argus As 8 engine, which made possible a much lower drag cowling, but was produced in just a few units. The factory then reverted to a radial, the 260hp, 470 cu. in., 7-cylinder Sienens-Halske Sh 14.

This powered the FW-44C, the main production version, of which an undetermined number was built and equipped almost every Luftwaffe primary training school. All the production FW-44s were actually built by Aero in Czechoslovakia for Germany, while others were built on license in Sweden (85 produced as the SK12 by what became SAAB), with almost half going to the Finnish Air Force. Still others were built in Argentina, Brazil, Austria and Bulgaria.

One of the oddest uses to which any World War II trainer was put was as the fuselage of a prototype helicopter built by Heinrich Focke. It eventually was developed into the FW-61, a machine with rotors on outriggers, Germany's first truly successful rotary-wing aircraft, though it never went into quantity production.

Specifications

Length: 23ft 11in
Wingspan: 29ft 6in
Height: 9ft 2in
Wing area: 215 sq ft
Empty weight: 1,245lb
Maximum speed: 115mph

Maximum range: 340 miles
Service ceiling: 12,790ft
Rate of climb: 3,360ft/min.

Surviving Examples

FW-44J
c/n 2816, Fv 5773 – Aerospace Museum, Stockholm
Fv 2827 – Pima Air & Space Museum
Ee122 – Museo Nacionale de Aeronautica, Buenos Aires, Argentina

Arado Ar-79

A casual observer strolling up to an Ar-79 should be excused from assuming it was an early postwar touring airplane. Its clean lines, smooth wing surface and retractable landing gear would certainly point in the direction of speedy cross-country transportation, and not toward military training and liaison flying. Still, the latter were the uses to which most of the few little Arados were consigned to by the German Air Ministry.

It was built in a most modern way for a touring airplane. The fuselage had a steel tube basic structure which supported a monocoque rear covering, with only the portion between the cockpit and cowling covered with fabric. The wings were of wood with fabric over the smooth plywood skin.

In fact, the job at which the Ar-79 truly excelled was record-setting. Within a few months in 1938, the first prototype set an FAI class mark with a 1,000km flight at 142mph, and the second prototype set a mark for 2,000km at 141mph. A few months later, a third example, with large auxiliary fuel tanks, was flown 3,917

Wing area: 151 sq ft
Empty weight: 1,015lb
Maximum speed: 143mph
Maximum range: 635 miles
Service ceiling: 18,040 ft
Rate of climb: 1,100ft/min

Surviving Example

Flying Legends Deutschland

Italy

Nardi FN.305

This sporty-looking low-wing monoplane with fully retractable landing gear was one of the few Italian advanced trainers designed for that purpose. The first one flew in January 1939 as a tandem two-seater with a closed canopy and a 200hp Fiat A.70S engine, which was soon replaced with an 185hp inline, air-cooled Alfa Romeo 115 engine, converting it into a 305A.

Next came prototypes of the two intended production versions: a single-seat fighter trainer with an open cockpit, and a two-seat basic trainer, also with an open cockpit, as the Italian air force was still flying open-cockpit combat airplanes.

The FN.305A was chosen as the standard Italian military trainer, 258 being ordered in 1938 from Piaggio, as the Nardi factory was too small to cope with such a large order. Some of these airplanes were built as open-cockpit FN.305Cs and others as closed-cockpit FN.305Ds.

miles non-stop from Libya to India at 100mph. All of this was achieved on just the 100hp of a Hirth HM 504 A-2 four-cylinder engine.

Just why an airplane with such performance was chosen as a trainer and then used for utility purposes is unknown.

Specifications

Length: 25ft 0in
Wingspan: 32ft 10in
Height: 6ft 11in

Specifications

Length: 22ft 11in
Wingspan: 27ft 10in
Height: 6ft 11in
Wing area: 129 sq ft
Empty weight: 1,550lb
Maximum speed: 185mph
Maximum range: 385 miles
Service ceiling: 19,685 ft

Surviving Examples

Italian Air Force MM52757 – Italian Air Force Museum, Vigna di
  Valle
c/n 87 – National Military Museum, Bucharest, Rumania

Once the domestic order had been filled, Nardi went into the export business, contracting with the French for a large number, but only delivering 41 before the two countries found themselves at war. Other orders included 9 for Chile, 31 for Hungary and 50 for to be built on license in Rumania. Hungary ordered 50.

The FN.305D was a special long-range version with a 285hp Czechoslovakian-built 9-cylinder Walter Bora radial engine, and used for long-distance record attempts. A two-seater was flown non-stop from Italy to Ethiopia in March 1939 for an FAI Class record of 2,774 miles. A single- seater went to Yugoslavia for a planned east-west trans-Atlantic flight, but was never used.

Saiman 202M

This was another sport airplane pressed into service as a military trainer in a move that was expedient, if not wholly successful. The first 202 was test-flown in early 1938 by Mario de Bernardi, one of Italy's great speed pilots and winner of the 1926 Schneider Cup Race. It was powered by a 120hp deHavilland Gypsy Major 4-cylinder, air-cooled, inline engine. It had a closed cabin and seating for two, side-by-side, as was becoming common for airplanes aimed at the pilot who wishes to share the enjoyment of flying with a friend.

The production version – the 202bis – used a 4-cylinder, inverted inline, air-cooled Alfa Romeo 110 engine, which had been modeled after the Gypsy. A special 202/I, with a slightly higher horsepower Alfa, was entered in a military trainer competition in 1939, and

Maximum speed: 137mph
Maximum range: 375 miles
Service ceiling: 16,500ft

Surviving Examples

MM52161 – Aviation Museum, Rimini
MM52163 – Caproni Aeronautical Museum, Milan

Ambrosini S.7

The S.7 looks like an airplane designed primarily for speed, and that is exactly what it was. Its intended market was purely civilian, as it had few qualities that would have made it useful for any purpose other than high-speed touring and record-setting. It was certainly not intended to be a trainer.

won a contract for 365 airplanes, which reverted to the standard Alfa 110. A single example of the 202R (or 204) had four seats and a 195hp Alfa Romeo 6-cylinder, inline, air-cooled engine of 561 cu. in. piston displacement.

After the war, the surviving 202s were sold to sporting pilots and the type returned to its roots.

Specifications

Length: 25ft 6in
Wingspan: 35ft 0in
Height: 6ft 3in
Wing area: 190 sq ft
Empty weight: 1,480lb

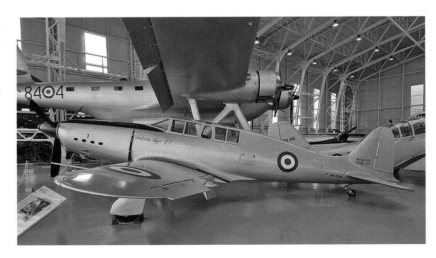

Powering the beautifully streamlined Ambrosini monoplane was a 270hp Hirth HM.508D inverted inline, air-cooled V-8 engine of 8 liters piston displacement. When the modified S.7 went into limited production (only 10 built) as a two-seat military trainer in 1943, it used a 180hp Isotta-Fraschini S.A.I.7 V-8. They remained in use by the Reggia Aeronautica until 1956.

The first target of the two prototypes was a major competition for touring airplanes, to be held just a short time after they first flew. While neither won the event, due in great part to a serious lack of flight testing, one of them just a few weeks later set an FAI class record for a 100km. closed-course flight at an official 251mph.

After the war, the S.7 with an Alfa Romeo engine, went into series production, with most of the 145 produced being used for flight training. In addition, several were used for more record-setting, such as the 1,000km mark set in 1951 at 223mph. Many can still be seen at private airfields in Italy and elsewhere.

Specifications

Length: 27ft 10in
Wingspan: 29ft 10in
Height: 9ft 2in
Wing area: 138 sq ft
Empty weight: 2,435lb
Maximum speed: 222mph
Maximum range: 620 miles
Service ceiling: 17,200ft

Surviving Example

I-PAIN – Milan

Japan

Tachikawa Ki.55

In 1943, the Tachikawa Ki.36 "Ida" Army cooperation airplane was pulled out of combat areas as it had proven an easy victim of Allied fighters. As the design had shown good flying qualities, the surviving airplanes were returned to Japanese-held sections of China to serve as Ki.55 advanced trainers, a capacity in which they performed well.

The original Ki.36 dated back to its first flight in 1938, powered by a 450hp Hitachi He.13 radial engine. As long as the Chinese had opposed them in mid-1930s fighters, they were able to carry out their assignments. Operating them from captured island bases exposed them to more modern airplanes.

By the time production ended in 1944, more than 1,300 had been built.

Specifications

Length: 26ft 3in
Wingspan: 39ft 9in
Height: 12ft 11in
Wing area: 215 sq ft
Empty weight: 2,850lb
Maximum speed: 217mph
Maximum range: 660 miles
Service ceiling: 26,900ft

Surviving Example

Bangkok

Mansyu Ki.79 "Nate"

When part or all of another country's territory was captured by Japan during World War II, it was often absorbed into the Japanese Empire and treated as a permanent possession. This was true first in the case of the occupation of Manchuria, and later with Singapore, Java, The Phillippines and other lands.

In Manchuria, the Japanese established the first and only airplane factory in that country. Mansyu began operation in 1942 building the Ki.79 advanced trainer version of the Army's Ki.27 "Nate" on license from Nakajima.

There were four versions of the Ki.79. The "a" sub-type was an all-metal single-seat trainer powered by a 510hp Hitachi Ha.13a-1 radial engine. The "b" was a two-seat "a". The "c" sub-type had a mixed construction of wood and metal to conserve scarce aluminum; it was a single-seat trainer with an up-dated Hitachi Ha.13a-III engine. The "d" sub-type was a two-seat version of the "c". All were assigned to flying schools in captured territories.

When production ended, more than 1,300 had been built. Some served after the war in Indonesia's war of independence from the Netherlands, and the Communist take-over of China.

Specifications

Length: 25ft 2in
Wingspan: 37ft 9in
Height: 9ft 10in
Wing area: 200 sq ft
Empty weight: 2,860lb
Maximum speed: 211mph
Maximum range: 580 miles
Service ceiling: 18,350ft
Rate of climb: 1,750ft/min

Surviving Example

Indonesia

Tachikawa Ki.9 "Spruce"

It was seen as Japan's most important primary and basic trainer during the late-1930s build-up to World War II. The original plan was to use two very different engines in the same airframe in order for them to perform the different duties of the first airplane to be flown by novice pilots, and also an airplane that could take the successful of the rookies into the more advanced demands of basic training.

As should have been realized, extensive modifications to the airframe would have to accompany the changes in power. For

the primary trainer, they chose the 112hp, 7-cylinder, air-cooled Nakajima NZ engine, and for the more advanced flight training program it would be replaced by the 350hp, 9-cylinder Hitachi Ha-13a engine. This simple increase in weight would throw the airplane out of balance unless other changes were made at the same time.

As it turned out, the change in airframe weight produced a shift in the center of gravity, and thus to the airplane's stability, which is of great significance when it was being flown by pilots with very little experience. Good judgment prevailed and the primary trainer was canceled.

After adapting the design to changes dictated by the results of the testing program, it went into production in 1935 at a low rate. In 1939, as the war with China escalated and more trainers were needed for the expanding Imperial Japanese Army Air Force, the

early production version was simplified and lightened. Many of the Model C were equipped with a standard collapsible blind-flying hood for instrument training.

By the time air force production ended in 1942, more than 2,600 had been delivered. After the war, some of the remaining airplanes found their way to the Indonesian Air Force and the air force of Shiang Kai-Shek which was increasingly busy with the Communist insurgents.

Specifications

Length: 25ft 11in
Wingspan: 33ft 10in
Height: 10ft 2in
Wing area: 264 sq ft
Empty weight: 2,470lb
Maximum speed: 150mph
Maximum range: 325 miles
Service ceiling: 19,000ft

Surviving Examples

Indonesia

Yokosuka K5Y "Willow"

It was the Japanese Navy's counterpart to the Army's Ki.9 and bore a superficial resemblance to the USAAF's Stearman PT-17. It was Japan's most important basic trainer from its introduction in 1934 until the end of the war in 1945. Barely 1 per cent of the 5,770 produced came from the Kawanishi factory, where some redesign

guns, one fixed and firing forward, and the other flexible and mounted in the rear cockpit.

All were powered by the Hitachi Amakaze 11 9-cylinder, air-cooled radial engine rated at 300hp. An advanced K5Y4 version with a 480hp Amakaze 21A was planned, but never built, nor was a K5Y5 with a 515hp Amakaze 15 engine. Both would have been land-based.

Specifications

Length: 26ft 5in
Wingspan: 36ft 1in
Height: 10ft 6in
Wing area: 298 sq ft
Empty weight: 2.200lb
Maximum speed: 130mph
Maximum range: 635 miles
Service ceiling: 18,700 ft
Rate of climb: 735ft/min

Surviving Example

Museum Abu Satriamandala, Indonesia

work had been done immediately prior to production, and none at all from the originators of the airplane, Yokosuka.

The immediate predecessor of the K5Y was the Yokosuka Type 91, but the prototypes suffered from instability and had to undergo numerous changes before being accepted as the K5Y1 in 1933. The first ones were built with conventional wheeled landing gear, but the later K5Y2 and K5Y3 were equipped with twin floats. Both styles were capable of some difficult aerobatic maneuvers. For realistic combat training, all versions carried two .30 cal. machine

Chapter 3
Reconnaissance/Observation/Scout

Observing an enemy from the air was the first use of aircraft for military purposes, the initial event having been in France in 1794. An airplane was first used for such purposes in 1911 in Italy, and in the early part of World War I it was the single- and two-seat scout planes that opened the modern era of military aviation. It was only when the effectiveness of observing from above had become apparent that pursuits and then bombers entered the fray.

These, along with captive balloons, were the eyes of the fleets and the armies, ranging out from their home bases on daring solo missions to locate the enemy's forces and rescue their own aircrew who had been forced down by bullets, flak, lack of fuel or mechanical failure. For the men who had been saved, their pilots deserved every medal and commendation they received.

Almost always too slow and too lightly armed to permit air-to-air combat, they flew low or near clouds or with an escort of pursuit planes for protection until over friendly territory. As technology improved, special cameras augmented the observer's eyes and his notebook, enabling a permanent record of the enemy's forces to be made.

Scientists and engineers soon took over, enabling observations to be made at high speed and high altitude, eventually reaching a previously unimagined level of sophistication with the use of radar and orbiting spacecraft which could produce results of amazing detail in real time.

United States of America

Vought OS2U Kingfisher

If not for a spectacular rescue, the Kingfisher might have lingered in relative obscurity outside the U.S. Navy, which operated most of them. Eight men, including America's top ace of World War I, Captain Eddie Rickenbacker, were picked up from their life rafts after their transport had crashed and they had drifted for almost three weeks.

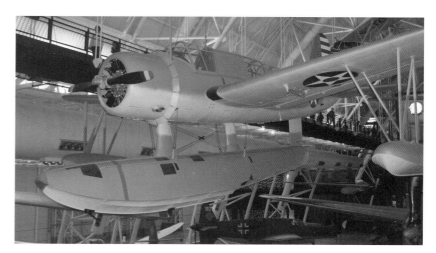

The Kingfisher was the U.S. Navy's first all-metal monoplane reconnaissance airplane, available with either wheels in order to operate from aircraft carriers or and bases, or floats to be catapulted off battleships and cruisers and recovered by crane.

The prototype Vought factory model VS.310 flew on the power of a 450hp Pratt & Whitney R-985 single-row, air-cooled Wasp Jr in March 1938. The first order for 54 airplanes was slow to be filled, the first OS2U-1s being delivered in the summer of 1940. A contract for another 158, designated US2U-2, followed after minor improvements.

The main production version – OS2U-3 – had the same basic P&W engine, along with self-sealing fuel tanks and increased armor plating. Two .30 cal. machine guns were installed, one in the nose

and the other to be operated by the rear-most crew member. For offensive purposes, this model could carry a 325lb. depth charge for anti-submarine use, as well as a single 100lb bomb. slung under either wing.

In addition to their primary purpose, they delivered precious mail from home to lonely GIs fighting bugs and snakes, as well as the enemy, at radio, radar and weather stations on little islands scattered around the South Pacific.

The operational lifetime of the Kingfisher was extended beyond projections when its intended replacement – the Curtiss SO3C-1 Seagull – failed to live up to performance guarantees due to a lack of horsepower from its Ranger inverted V-12 engine. As the war wore on, Curtiss' new radial-engined SC-1 Seahawk finally edged the Kingfisher into second-line jobs.

In an effort to improve its take-off and landing performance, the experimental XOS2U-4 was tried with higher aspect-ratio wings and full-span flaps, but never went into production. Of the 1,519 built, 300 were called the OS2N-1, having been built at the Naval Aircraft Factory.

Specifications

Length: 33ft 10in on floats
Wingspan: 35ft11in
Height: 15ft 2in
Wing area: 262 sq ft
Empty weight: 4,125lb
Maximum speed: 165mph
Maximum range: 800 miles
Service ceiling: 13,000ft
Rate of climb: 950ft/min

Surviving Examples

OS2U
Fighter Factory

OS2U-3
BuAer 5909 – U.S. National Air & Space Museum
BuAer 5925 – National Aviation Museum, Santiago, Chile
BuAer 5926 – U.S. National Museum of Naval Aviation

OS2U-4
BuAer 0951 – Battleship *Alabama*,

Douglas O-38F

For many years the U.S. Army relied on Douglas airplanes to perform its reconnaissance missions. From the O-2 with its 435hp Liberty V-12 of World War I vintage, to the O-25 of 1930 with its 600hp Curtiss V-12, to the O-38 with its 525hp Pratt & Whitney R-1690 Hornet radial engine, the same basic airframe carried pilots and observers during their working hours.

The first of 44 O-38s, identified by their short-chord Townend engine cowls, were delivered in 1931 to National Guard squadrons. Next came a single unarmed O-38A used as a staff liaison airplane, also for the National Guard. A slightly later version of the Hornet engine marked the next production version – the O-38B – 30 of which went to Army Air Corps units and 33 to the National Guard. One O-38C, similar to the O-38B, went to the U.S. Coast Guard. With relatively few airplanes going to front line units, it would appear that scouting and observation were not considered of prime importance during peacetime.

Major changes went into the O-38E, including an enlarged fuselage with a sliding canopy over what had been two open cockpits, and a 625hp version of the Hornet engine. There was a choice of operating them on floats, as well as wheels, but all 37 of them went to the National Guard. Eight O-38Fs were National Guard staff liaison planes which lacked guns. This brought the total O-38s produced for domestic consumption to 146, of which more than 80 per cent went to National Guard squadrons.

For offensive purposes, most O-38s were armed with a single .30 cal. machine gun firing forward, and another on a flexible mount and used by the backseat observer. In addition, up to four 100lb bombs could be carried.

Specifications

Length: 32ft 0in
Wingspan: 40ft 0in
Height: 10ft 8in
Wing area: 371 sq ft
Empty weight: 3,070lb
Maximum speed: 150mph
Maximum range: 565 miles
Service ceiling: 19,750ft
Rate of climb: 950ft/min

Surviving Example

USAAC 33-324– National Museum of the U.S. Air Force

Douglas O-46A

The last dedicated observation airplane built by Douglas was distinctive, being one of the very few parasol monoplanes used by the U.S. military. Unfortunately, as a first-line airplane, it was far from a success, even though its downward visibility was superior to its predecessors.

It followed the U.S. Army's rigid thinking which had changed little since World War I, and called for large, heavy, powerful recce airplanes that were meant to fly off well prepared runways that were well back from the front lines. America's first effort to simulate the emerging changes in the way battles were going to be fought in the next war was the 1939 Army Maneuvers, which involved much of the slowly growing forces.

The older airplanes were too heavy and clumsy to cope with the changes, which led to the introduction of small, light modified

two-seat personal airplanes like Piper's classic J-3 Cub. They could fly in and out of almost any clearing, and evade much faster enemy fighters with their maneuverability. Moreover, they could be flown by infantry officers with just a few hours training.

The O-46 prototype, which flew in 1935, was an O-43 with modified wing bracing and a 700hp Pratt & Whitney Twin Wasp Jr radial engine in place of the Curtiss inverted V-12 of only slightly less power. The U.S. Army Air Corps ordered just 90 airplanes, few of which left the U.S.A. Several were flown by National Guard units on anti-submarine patrol.

A planned follow-on, the O-48, was to have used a 775hp Wright R-1670 radial engine, but was never built.

Specifications

Length: 34ft 7in
Wingspan: 45ft 9in
Height: 10ft 9in
Wing area: 332 sq ft
Empty weight: 4,775lb
Maximum speed: 200mph
Maximum range: 435 miles
Service ceiling: 24,150ft
Rate of climb: 1,765ft/min

Surviving Example

USAAC 35-179 – National Museum of the U.S. Air Force

North American O-47

It was a modern airplane designed to an out-dated requirement. It was an all-metal, three-place, mid-wing with retractable landing gear and a three-bladed metal propeller. The prototype XO-47 was built and flown in 1936 by what would soon become North American Aviation. Had there been a need for a large, heavy, none-too-maneuverable observation airplane, it would not doubt have served that purpose well.

But the day of such airplanes was ending, though few seem to have realized this at the time. The Army Air Corps ordered 164 O-47As in 1937, powered by a single 975hp 9-cylinder Wright R-1820 Cyclone 9. More than half went to Army squadrons, the rest being for various state National Guard units. Two years later, another 74 were ordered of the O-47B with an up-rated Wright Cyclone and an additional fuel tank to deal with the increased consumption.

It was the extensive training maneuvers of 1941 that revealed major weaknesses in such large airplanes that were unable to

cope with rapidly changing battle fronts and relegated several of the latest observation types to support duties, while some of their functions were assumed by a series of slightly modified, highly nimble and adaptable personal airplanes; the need for high-performance recce airplanes was being filled by re-equipped fighters and light bombers.

Most of the 239 O-47s were put to work patrolling the Atlantic and Pacific Coast for Axis submarines until replaced as soon as better airplanes became available.

Specifications

Length: 33ft 7in
Wingspan: 46ft 4in
Height: 12ft 2in
Wing area: 350 sq ft
Empty weight: 5,980lb
Maximum speed: 220mph
Maximum range: 840 miles
Service ceiling: 23,200ft
Rate of climb: 1,470ft/min

Surviving Examples

O-47A
USAAC 37-279 – U.S. National Air & Space Museum
USAAC 37-??? – Planes of Fame

O-47B
USAAC 39-098 – Combat Air Museum, Topeka, Kansas
USAAC 39-112 – National Museum of the U.S. Air Force

Curtiss O-52 Owl

The Owl symbolized the era of heavy observation airplanes that were forced to surrender their place as low-altitude army cooperation airplanes to thousands of Piper Cubs and Aeronca Champions that had fueled a great boom in inexpensive two-seat personal airplanes toward the end of the Great Depression. At the other end of the scale – high-speed and high-altitude photo-reconnaissance – the load was transferred to such as Lockheed P-38 Lightning long-range fighters that carried cameras in place of machine guns in the nose.

The O-52 had no direct predecessor, nor was there a true prototype. A single order for 203 airplanes was placed in 1940. Their fatal weaknesses were seen in realistic war games when what would become known as liaison types hopped in and out of spaces no larger than baseball diamonds or cricket pitches, while flown by quickly trained pilots, many of whom had flown Cubs and Champs as civilians.

All that was left for the Owls was patrolling along the ocean coasts for submarines, while small factories began churning out more than 10,000 of what the GIs called "grasshoppers".

An improbable order for 30 Owls came from the U.S.S.R., though they used just 10 of them for artillery spotting and photo-recce jobs.

Specifications

Length: 26ft 4in
Wingspan: 40ft 9in
Height: 9ft 3in
Wing area: 210 sq ft
Empty weight: 4,200lb
Maximum speed: 220mph

The standard Navy airplane was among the first to be fitted with amphibious floats and fully-retractable wheels and built as the first product of the new Grumman Aircraft Co. The O3U could thus operate with equal facility from aircraft carriers, airfields and bodies of water. Almost 290 were built for the U.S. and scores more for seven other countries mainly in South America, but including both Germany and Japan.

The U.S. never used either the O2U or O3U in combat, but other countries did, including Mexico, Peru and China. The 140 Corsairs still with the U.S. Navy at the start of World War II were all in minor roles where they would not face enemy airplanes having far greater performance.

The sole surviving original Corsair was part of a group of 32 built for Thailand.

Maximum range: 700 miles
Service ceiling: 21,000ft

Surviving Example

USAAC 40-2746 – Pima Air & Space Museum
USAAC 40-2763 – National Museum of the U.S. Air Force
USAAC 40-2769 – Yanks Air Museum, Chino, California

Vought O3U-6 Corsair

The first U.S. Navy airplane to be named Corsair was the Vought O2U scout/observation biplane, of which 580 were built, with deliveries starting in 1927. By 1930, the improved O3U was being built with an uprated Pratt & Whitney R-1340 Wasp, which would ultimately power many thousands of North American AT-6/Harvard advanced trainers.

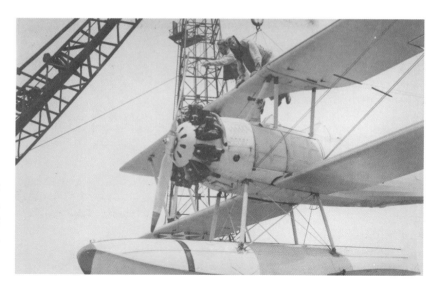

Specifications

Length: 27ft 6in
Wingspan: 36ft 0in
Height: 11ft 4in
Wing area: 337 sq ft
Empty weight: 3,200lb
Maximum speed: 167mph
Maximum range: 680 miles
Service ceiling: 18,600ft

Surviving Example

Thai Air Force Museum

Great Britain

Supermarine Stranraer

The Royal Air Force had a long and proud history of operating large biplane flying boats, which was coming to an end as World War II approached. With one last effort, it ordered 17 Stranraers, the final such design to come from the legendary R.J. Mitchell. It was to be used for coastal reconnaissance.

The prototype, which flew in 1934, powered by two 820hp, sleeve-valve Bristol Pegasus IIIM radial engines, used metal extensively in its structure and was covered with sheet aluminum alloy except for the wings, which used fabric. In August 1935, 17 were ordered with 920hp Pegasus X engines, the first flying in December 1936.

From the start, the Stranraer came up short in both speed and range, when compared with other large seaplanes being readied for the same functions. Still, they entered operational service in April 1937. It isn't clear if an additional six that were ordered were ever delivered. Construction of 40 was begun in 1940 by Canadian Vickers and they were to be operated by the RCAF.

When the war began, 15 remained in RAF service, though they had been rendered obsolete by the arrival of the Sunderland, which offered greater speed, range and offensive weaponry. The desperate need for patrol seaplanes to escort convoys and search for U-boats was such that Stranraers continued to be used until late 1940, when they were relegated to training crews for the newer boats.

The Canadian-built flying boats were kept in service until 1944, and many were then sold to private operators, one of whom re-engined theirs with 1,000hp Wright R-1820 engines. The last one is said to have been retired in 1957.

Specifications

Length: 54ft 10in
Wingspan: 85ft 0in
Height: 21ft 9in
Wing area: 1,457 sq ft
Empty weight: 11,250lb
Maximum speed: 165mph
Maximum range: 1,000 miles
Service ceiling: 18,500ft
Rate of climb: 1,350ft/min

Surviving Example

m/s 920 – RAF Museum, Hendon

Union of Soviet Socialist Republics

Polikarpov R-5

From the end of World War I until well into World War II, Nikolay Polikarpov was responsible for almost all Soviet trainers, fighters and reconnaissance airplanes, starting with a version of the deHavilland 9 which was the first mass produced Soviet airplane, and including those built from 1929 to 1933 when he was in prison on trumped-up charges. The R-5 replaced the dH.9 as the leading reconnaissance bomber from 1928 and serving the Red Air Force through major battles of 1939–1940 and then reverting to night operations through 1944.

The prototype R-5 flew in 1928 with an imported (captured?) German 680hp BMW inverted V-12, and went into production after a long period of development in 1930 with license-built BMWs. Along with military versions, the P-5 airliner version was built for Aeroflot even though it could carry but two passengers or 900lb of cargo.

The R-5 first saw combat in the Spanish Civil War from 1936, then in the 1939 fighting against Japan over Mongolia. Use in the initial Winter War with Finland in 1939–1940 followed. Versatility was forced on the R-5 by the lack of alternatives. But it seemed to be adaptable to a variety of uses despite its outdated design.

Civil versions, too, served long past the time when they should have been retired, as they were available in large numbers and were rugged enough for the difficult conditions. Some received closed cabins, and others carried novel (and no doubt bitterly uncomfortable) containers under the wings for as many as seven passengers. A few continued in use after the war until they could be replaced by even slightly more modern airplanes. In all, at least 6,000 were built.

Specifications

Length: 34ft 8in
Wingspan: 50ft 10in
Height: 10ft 8in
Wing area: 540 sq ft
Empty weight 4,340lb
Maximum speed: 142mph
Maximum range: 500 miles
Service ceiling: 21,000ft
Rate of climb: 1,500ft/min

Surviving Example

Monino

Germany

Blohm & Voss BV.138 Sea Dragon

It was Nazi Germany's primary long-range maritime patrol airplane, yet fewer than 300 were built in a 5–6 year production run. It was heavily armed with two 20mm cannon (1 each in the bow and stern turrets), as well as three .30 cal. machine guns and one .50 cal. machine gun (in the rear of the upper engine nacelle). While its cruising range enabled it to extend far from its home

base, its cruising speed of no more than 150mph must have made it easy prey for Allied fighters and even light bombers.

The first prototype of what was originally called the Ha-138 was flown in July 1937, followed by the second a month later and were aimed at developing a long-range airliner for transatlantic service. After numerous proving flights, that plan was dropped in favor of a military seaplane for the planned coming war. Three prototypes of the BV-138 were powered by a variety of engines ranging from 650 to 1,000hp each. The 880hp Junkers Jumo 205D diesel engine was selected for the production machines.

The first BV-138C entered service in March 1941, a year and a half later, and could carry up to 1,100lb of depth charges or high-explosive bombs, with 227 of the total of 297 examples built. Most operated off the water, but some were catapulted off seaplane tenders. Much of their missions were in co-operation with U-Boats, in the search for Allied merchant ships.

On surveillance operations, they were used as far north as the Arctic Ocean, and as far south as the Mediterranean Sea. The only survivor is a battered example that was sunk in July 1945 during an air show demonstration in Denmark when RAF fighter-bombers used it as a target. It was not raised until 2000 during preparations for construction of a major bridge.

Specifications

Length: 65ft 4in
Wingspan: 88ft 7in
Height: 21ft 8in
Wing area: 1,205 sq ft
Empty weight: 17,850lb
Maximum speed: 170mph
Maximum range: 3,100 miles
Service ceiling: 16,400ft
Rate of climb: 730ft/min

Surviving Example

Luftwaffe NJ+HE – Danish Tecnik Museum, as recovered

Focke Wulf FW.189

Developed initially as an observation airplane having unusually broad visibility, it was later used for a variety of missions, including a dual-control trainer, VIP transport and ground attack, with appropriate modifications.

It resulted from a 1937 specification for a single-engined recce airplane, but was accepted with a pair of 450hp, 7-litre, air-cooled Argus 410 inverted V-12 engines, as one of the few twin-boom designs to become operational in any air force. The almost 850 delivered were built in Germany, then occupied France and finally occupied Czechoslovakia.

The FW-189 was used mainly on the Eastern Front, where it displayed an ability to avoid attacking Soviet fighters with its excellent maneuverability at low speed which could not be matched by its enemies.

For defensive use, the main production version – FW-189A-1 – had two .30 cal. machines fired by the middle of the three crew members, and two more by the man in the back seat. There were single machine guns in the wing roots for offensive purposes.

Developments of the A series included the FW-189B trainer, of which only 13 were built, and the FW-189F, which had two 690hp

Argus 411 V-12s. Other proposed but not built versions were the FW-189C ground-attack airplane, and the FW-189D twin-float seaplane.

Specifications

Length: 39ft 4in
Wingspan: 60ft 4in
Height: 12ft 0in
Wing area: 409 sq ft
Empty weight: 5,900lb
Maximum speed: 222mph
Maximum range: 415 miles
Service ceiling: 27,550ft
Rate of climb: 1,640ft/min

Surviving Example

Paine Field, Everett, Washington

Junkers Ju.388

The Ju.88 was not only Germany's finest medium bomber of the war, but one of the very best from any nation. It was developed into many special-purpose versions, including one purely for high-altitude reconnaissance: the Ju.388, which started out to be a fast interceptor that could take on the Boeing B-29s expected to be operating from England.

The appearance at an RAF base of a service test YB-29 in late 1942 caused panic in the German Air Ministry, as its latest fighters could not perform well at the unprecedented altitudes for which the B-29 was designed. A high-altitude version of the Ju.88 lacked the speed and rate of climb needed to deal with the sleek, powerful Superfortress.

A test version called the Ju.188J was tried with three different engines, the most promising of which never got beyond the experimental stage. When versions with the other engines were fully equipped for combat with radar and other appendages, their performance dropped below what was needed. The first true prototype of the Ju.388 flew in December 1943, and the first was delivered to squadrons in August, 1944, by which time it had become obvious that they would have no B-29s to chase.

The use of the Ju.388 for reconnaissance suffered greatly from the slow delivery of engines, the effective bombing of the production facilities and the rapidly improving high-altitude performance of Allied fighters. As with many Luftwaffe airplanes, the Ju.388 might have done what it had been designed for, had it been available when it was needed.

However, had the European part of the war continued much longer, and Germany remained a feared opponent, B-29s may well have been used to drop nuclear weapons on Germany, as that was the original aim of the Manhattan Project.

Specifications

Length: 49ft 10.5in
Wingspan: 72ft 2in
Height: 14ft 3in
Wing area: 603 sq ft
Empty weight: 22,930lb
Maximum speed: 383mph
Maximum range: 1,415 miles

Service ceiling: 44,100ft
Rate of climb: 1,240ft/min

Surviving Example of the Ju.388L

Luftwaffe 560049 – U.S. National Air & Space Museum

Arado Ar-196

The limited view of a distant enemy afforded a sailor on a capital ship's deck was first extended by placing a lookout atop a tall mast. The next step was to make use of the airplane's ability to climb thousands of feet into the sky and see far beyond the limited horizon of those near the surface. When far at sea, such a ship could not avail itself of the "eyes" of range-limited land-based airplanes and so needed its own flying machines.

The obvious answer was to develop scouting airplanes that could be launched by catapult from cruisers and battleships wherever they might be sailing. One of the very best of these was the Arado Ar-196, as many as four of which were carried by some of Germany's largest battleships.

By the early 1930s the Heinkel He-60 float-equipped biplane was paving the way for the development of this weapon, but it lacked the needed performance.

Enter the He-114 with the first of an historic series of Daimler Benz 600-series inverted V-12 engines, the DB.600, of 1,000hp. But this seaplane, too, was far from a success, as the new engine was not available in sufficient numbers and so was replaced by an 800hp BMW 132 radial. This produced little more speed than the seaplane it was meant to replace, and the He-114's water handling was considerable worse.

In 1936, the German Air Ministry announced its need for yet another scout to be powered by the BMW engine, as the demand for the superior DB 600 and its developments was to be reserved for the forthcoming Messerschmitt 109 and 110 fighters and the He-111 bomber. Most of the designs offered for the new airplane were biplanes, aside from Arado's Ar-196.

The single- and twin-float prototypes flew in 1937, with the former going into production in late 1938. Defensive armament was limited to a single .30 cal. machine gun operated by the observer in the rear seat. This was replaced in late 1939, by an improved version armed with two fixed-firing 20 mm cannon and a machine gun, all firing forward for offensive purposes. It could carry a pair of 110lb bombs under the wings.

While its pilots liked the Arado for shipboard operations, the steady loss of large surface ships to Allied attacks meant that they were switched to coastal patrol from land bases. The Ar-196 was considered one of the very best of the wartime small reconnaissance seaplanes.

Specifications

Length: 36ft 1in
Wingspan: 40ft 0in
Height: 14ft 7in
Wing area: 306 sq ft
Empty weight: 6,590lb
Maximum speed: 193mph
Maximum range: 670 miles
Service ceiling: 23,000ft
Rate of climb: 980ft / min

Surviving Examples

Ar.196A

Ar9643 – Museum of Aviation & the Air Force, Plovdiv, Bulgaria
Luftwaffe PO+HG – U.S. National Air & Space Museum

Italy

Meridionali Ro.37 Lince (Lynx)

In 1934, the Romeo firm took over Meriodionali and then changed its name to Meridionali while retaining the Ro (Romeo) designation for its later airplanes. The first of these was the Ro-37 two-seat recce-fighter, a conventional biplane with fixed, faired landing gear. Power was from a 600hp, inverted V-12 Fiat A.30, which had a tendency to over-heat in warmer climes.

The Ro-37bis solved this problem with a choice of air-cooled 9-cylinder radials: a 560hp Piaggio P.IX or 700hp P.XR. Both the 37 and 37bis were accepted by the Reggia Aeronautica, pilots and mechanics, production extending to 160 for the former and 475 for the latter. Many of them were exported to countries in Europe, the Middle East and Latin America.

Both versions of the Ro-43 were used extensively in the Spanish Civil War and Italy's invasion of Abyssinia, the latter being against almost no opposition. When Italy became embroiled in World War II, almost 300 were still in first-line units, but as they became obsolescent, they were withdrawn from the North African fighting to be used for minor functions. By the latter part of 1943, when Italy joined the Allies, they had been retired.

Specifications

Length: 31ft 10in
Wingspan: 38ft 1in
Height: 11ft 6in
Wing area: 359 sq ft
Empty weight: 3,925lb
Maximum speed: 185mph

increasingly capable Allied fighters despite steady increases in its power.

The prototype, powered by two very well-cowled 900hp Mitsubishi Ha.26 14-cylinder, air-cooled radial engines, failed to reach the performance expected of it, While it would out-run the Army's Ki.43 Oscar and the Navy's A6M Zero, then Japan's newest and best fighters, and the Allies' Hurricane and Curtiss P-36, it was well known that much faster replacements such as the Spitfire and Lightning were on their way to the Pacific.

The main production Ki.46-II was given 1,050hp Mitsubishi Ha.102 engines with two-speed, two-stage superchargers, and soon after the prototype's first flight, achieved a top speed of 375mph. It remained in operational service to the end of the war, by which time almost 1,100 had been built.

Maximum range: 930 miles
Service ceiling: 21,665ft

Surviving Example

Ro.37bis
MM27050 – Italian Air Force Museum

Japan

Mitsubishi Ki.46 Dinah

Aerodynamically, it was one of the best airplanes developed in Japan in World War II. And while it started out as a superior high-speed reconnaissance airplane, it was gradually out-classed by the

The long-range outlook remained grim, as P-47 Thunderbolts and P-51 Mustangs roamed the skies at high and low altitudes over Japan's home islands and dwindling collection of captured island bases. The Ki.46-III appeared with 1,500hp Mitsubishi engines and was slightly faster and longer-ranged. Still, the Ki.46 could not defend itself against the six or eight .50 cal. machine guns of the Allied fighters.

Nevertheless, the altitude and speed superiority of the Dinah over anything else built by Japan led inevitably to plans to convert it into an interceptor that could challenge the growing numbers of fast, high-flying B-29s that were dropping thousands of tons of high-explosive and incendiary bombs in daylight raids. Armed with two 20mm cannon in the nose, it could have proven more than a nuisance to the Superfortress. Except that it was a poor gun platform due to instability.

As the bombing from 20,000 feet and higher was not considered accurate enough by the USAAF, the B-29s of the 20th Air Force were switched to lower-level night raids. Then, the Ki-46's lack of radar made interception difficult.

Specifications

Length: 36ft
Wingspan: 48ft 3in
Height: 12ft 9in
Wing area: 344 sq ft
Empty weight: 7,190lb
Maximum speed: 375mph
Maximum range: 1,340 miles
Service ceiling: 35,200 ft
Rate of climb: 1,460ft/min

Surviving Example

Ki.46-III
m/s 5439 – RAF Museum, Cosford

Nakajima C6N1 Saiun (Colored Cloud) "Myrt"

Among the major shortcomings that eventually led to Japan's defeat in World War II was the remarkable lack of flexibility of some of its leaders. Right to the end, Japan was building combat airplanes that lacked self-sealing fuel tanks and thus were prone to blazing up when hit by a few bullets. Though they had enough far-sighted designers, too many Japanese bombers and fighters were intended to cope with present Allied counterparts, rather than future developments of them.

In the case of reconnaissance airplanes, the Nakajima C6N had the potential to be an outstanding carrier-based airplane, but relied on an engine that never produced its advertised horsepower. When that was added to the lack of large aircraft carriers needed by this high-speed airplane, it had little chance of reaching its goal.

The C6N was an answer to a 1942 Imperial Navy need for a scout plane that would reach a speed of 400mph and a range of 2,000 miles. To achieve this with the limited power of contemporary engines, Nakajima first proposed two 1,000hp engines housed in the fuselage and driving wing-mounted propellers via articulated drive shafts. When the 2,000hp Homare engine looked like it would be available in time, the radical design was replaced with a conventional layout.

A high aspect-ratio wing was designed to permit flight at very high altitudes, but needed complex lift-increasing flaps in order to operate from carriers, with their limited decks. The first C6N flew in May 1943, and by the time they began coming off the assembly line in February 1944, most of the large carriers were resting on the ocean floor, forcing the airplanes to use land bases. Just as great a problem was the Homare engine, which produced barely 2/3rd the horsepower expected of it, and suffered from poor quality control at the factory, which resulted in substandard reliability in what should have been an important engine.

An attempt to convert the recce airplane into a much-needed night fighter was the C6N1-S, a single-seat machine that carried two 20mm cannon but no AI (Air Intercept) radar to locate its prey in the dark. While 463 were built and did some good work, it failed to live up to its promise, a trait it had in common with many late-war Japanese airplanes.

Specifications

Length: 36ft 1in
Wingspan: 41ft 0in
Height: 13ft 12in
Wing area: 274 sq ft
Empty weight: 6,545lb
Maximum speed: 380mph
Maximum range: 3,300 miles
Service ceiling: 35,250ft

Surviving Example

USAAF FE-4803 – U.S. National Air & Space Museum

Kawanishi H8K2 "Emily"

World War II was the hey-day of the large, majestic flying boat. And the end of the line. Most of the major combatants – Great Britain, the U.S.A., Japan, Italy and even France – all developed watercraft with four or more engines intended for long flights with heavy loads.

Japan's large flying boat program began with Kawanishi's H6K "Mavis", in answer to a 1934 Imperial Navy specification. A four-engined, parasol-winged craft, the prototype flew July 1936 with 840hp Nakajima 9-cylinder radial engines. Defensive armament was limited to three .30 cal. machine guns, while offensively it could carry two torpedoes or 2,200lb of bombs, all hung from wing bracing struts.

Later prototypes had more guns and 1,000hp Mitsubishi engines. The first production run, of almost identical seaplanes, was for 10 recce-bombers and two specially outfitted as VIP transports. The main production version, of which 127 were delivered, had more machine guns plus a 20mm cannon in the tail. When full-scale war broke out in the Pacific in late 1941, 64 "Mavis" were with operational units.

As the "Mavis" was entering service, its replacement – the H8K "Emily" – was already in production. With the fuel and cruising speed to perform patrols as long as 24 hours, however, some of the older seaplanes remained in use into 1942, conducting bombing raids on targets on South Pacific islands.

The newer seaplane was a marked departure from previous practice, and as modern as any flying boat used in the war. It had a cantilever high wing and a very clean basic design, with four 1,530hp Mitsubishi Mk.4A engines inspired by Pratt & Whitney technology. It was 50mph faster and could carry several thousand pounds more fuel and payload than its predecessor. Defensive

Wing area: 1,722 sq ft
Empty weight: 40,520lb
Maximum speed: 290mph
Maximum range: 4,440 miles
Service ceiling: 28,740ft

Surviving Example

c/n 426 – Naval Air Station, Kagoshima

Aichi E13A1 "Jake"

In the days before orbiting satellites and long-range radar, nautical reconnaissance of vast ocean areas was performed by long-range seaplanes, which traded off the speed and load-carrying capacity of land-based airplanes for endurance.

armament was increased to five 20mm cannon and five .30 cal. machine guns with which to fight off much faster and more maneuverable Allied fighters. It also carried early ocean search radar.

One of its first missions was a three-plane unit with an assignment for a follow-up raid on Pearl Harbor in March 1942. The first attempt was thwarted by thick clouds, the second by American naval forces waiting at the point selected for re-fueling by submarine. In view of the round-the-clock alert status at the huge naval base and the breaking of a major Japanese naval code, success of such a raid was highly doubtful.

Specifications

Length: 92ft 4in
Wingspan: 124ft 8in
Height: 30ft 0in

As the Japanese carrier force was being methodically obliterated, the Japanese relied evermore heavily on flying boats such as the "Emily' and floatplanes like "Jake".

The immediate forerunner of the E13A was Aichi's E12A, designed in response to a Navy need for a new recce seaplane with better performance than the current Kawanishi E7K. Along with the prototype E12A, Aichi offered a larger and more powerful version, the E13A, both of which first flew in 1938.

The rivals to what became "Jake" were not up to the performance needed for a future full of plans for conquest and expansion of the Japanese Empire. Starting in late 1940, three factories turned out E13As to a total of 1,418 which made it the most widely produced and used maritime recce seaplane in the Japanese Navy. Initially, they were used in the war against China and were based on cruisers and seaplane tenders that were able to launch them via catapults and retrieve them with cranes.

The first major mission to see E13As used in quantity was the December 1941 attack on the U.S. Naval and Army bases in Hawaii. Next came the Battle of Midway, where "Jake" crews failed to report the American carriers in time to prevent a major defeat.

By 1943, as many as 250 were carried by Japanese capital ships, with many others flying off land bases. As the war progressed and American Hellcats and Lightnings replaced the out-dated P-40s and Wildcats, the lack of self-sealing fuel tanks and effective armor for the crew doomed scores of "Jakes" to flaming destruction. Those surviving Aichis ended their days in suicide attacks on Allied ships.

Efforts to modernize the 1930s design included adding search radar, heavier guns and structural improvements. None of these reached operational status before the war ended.

Specifications

Length: 37ft 1in
Wingspan: 47ft7in
Height: 15ft 5in
Wing area: 387 sq ft
Empty weight: 5,825lb
Maximum speed: 234mph
Maximum range: 1,300 miles
Service ceiling: 28,500ft
Rate of climb: 1,600ft/min

Surviving Example

Kasedo Peace Museum, Kyushu

Chapter 4
Liaison/Utility

When in 1942 the U.S. Army Air Forces decided to do away with the O-for Observation category and replace it with the new L-for-Liaison designation, it was in recognition of the variety of uses to which observation airplanes were being put. "Liaison", from the military standpoint, was a very vague term which could be applied to almost anything that didn't seem to fit elsewhere.

Almost all the airplanes that were eventually classed as "liaison" were off-the-shelf personal airplanes that were modified no more than absolutely necessary to perform their new duties. Anyone familiar with current light planes would recognize their military counterparts despite the drab color schemes and bright insignias.

United States of America

Vultee L-1 Vigilant

When U.S. Army leaders saw the performance of a German Fieseler Fi.156 Storch they were forced to reevaluate their thinking about Army cooperation airplanes. The spindly-but-nimble airplane had been demonstrated at the Cleveland National Air Races, after which the pilot was invited to Wright Field. After a night of enthusiastic drinking, he passed out and his airplane was dismantled, carefully measured and photographed and then reassembled before he sobered up.

The first result of the newfound knowledge was Vultee's L-1, with much less emphasis on speed and range than utility, thanks to its larger wings and considerably less weight. Short-field performance, in particular, was far better with the L-1 than with its predecessors, the O-47 and O-52.

But the L-1 (originally called the YO-49) was just a stop-gap measure, with Ryan's YO-51 Dragonfly using more of the Storch's

slow-flight techniques, including elaborate wing flaps, as well as leading edge slots. The YO-51 was never accepted by the Army, as even better ideas prevailed. Despite its weight, the L-1 is said to have been able to maintain level flight at just over 30mph, and to have a landing roll of as little as 50 feet.

The prototype Vigilant flew in July 1940, with orders eventually totaling 324, which was a lot until war came even closer and the need for mass production became recognized. The first production order was for 142 O-49s, while the second was for the slightly longer O-49A. They were used in a wide variety of roles, including towing smaller gliders, spotting for the artillery, search and rescue and even delivering spies behind enemy lines. At least 30 were sent to the Royal Air Force as the Vigilant I and II, while a single example went to the U.S. Navy as a CQ-2 for controlling target drones.

Construction was conventional steel tube and fabric other than sheet metal ahead of the cockpit. Power was provided by a 295hp, 9-cylinder Lycoming R-680 air-cooled radial engine.

Specifications

Length: 34ft 3in
Wingspan: 50ft 11in
Height: 10ft 2in
Wing area: 329 sq ft
Empty weight: 2,670lb
Maximum speed: 122mph
Maximum range: 280 miles
Service ceiling: 12,800ft
Rate of climb: 400ft/min

Surviving Examples

USAAC 40-3102 (O-49) – Fantasy of Flight
USAAF 41-19039 – National Museum of the U.S. Air Force
USAAF 41-22124 – U.S. National Air & Space Museum

Taylorcraft L-2

The next step in the direction of converting standard light planes into liaison craft was the modification of Taylorcraft's popular Piper Cub rival from side-by-side seating to a tandem configuration. Compared with the stop-gap L-1, it was one-third the weight, smaller all around, and had just 65hp to the L-1's 295hp. All this resulted in an airplane that was much cheaper and quicker to produce and had the needed short-field performance.

The first Taylorcrafts were built as YO-57, which served as sort of a prototype, then the O-57 of which 20 were delivered, and finally the O-57A of which 336 were built, with a rear seat that could be turned to face backwards. All were powered by a 65hp air-cooled, horizontally-opposed four-cylinder Continental O-170 engine, and had more windows for improved side and rear visibility. The first two were re-designated L-2, and the third, L-2A.

More of the early versions were built, bringing the total to 546. Next came the L-2B, intended primarily for artillery spotting and the first major version, 490 being built. The L-2C through L-2L were impressed privately owned airplanes, most of the 44 being of the side-by-side seating variety. The final major version was the L-2M, which had a tighter fitting engine cowl and spoilers on the wings for even better low-speed flight. Nine hundred were built, meant to be used as very light cargo and personnel transports, ambulances and for miscellaneous duties requiring the ability to land on almost any relatively flat area, often close to the front lines.

Total production was 1,936 before it ended in 1943; by then the L-2s had been declared "operationally obsolete" and were kept in the U.S.A. mainly for training.

Specifications

Length: 22ft 9in
Wingspan: 35ft 5in
Height: 6ft 8in
Wing area: 181 sq ft
Empty weight: 875lb
Maximum speed: 92mph
Maximum range: 230–300 miles
Service ceiling: 12,000 ft
Rate of climb: 400–475ft/min

Surviving Examples

USAAF 43-26110 – Pima Air and Space Museum
USAAF 43-26753 – National Museum of the U.S. Air Force

Aeronca L-3

The U.S. Army was in a great hurry to acquire as many versatile little airplanes as possible for what little money that was available. The U.S. light plane industry, which had survived the Great Depression and was showing strong signs of life, had what was needed and soon found itself in the military airplane business.

Aeronca's Tandem Trainer became an Army O-58 with the addition of windows at the rear of the cabin, some simple air-to-ground radio equipment, and a quick coat of olive drab paint. Realistic tests during the 1941 Army maneuvers showed that the idea had considerable merit.

Orders were placed for 20 O-58A with a wider fuselage and then 335 L-35B with windows extending well aft of the trailing edge of the wing. When the "O" series was changed to "L" a few months after the U.S.A. entered the war, all became L-3B's. To these were added 540 more L-5Bs, 490 L-3Bs and 490 L-3Cs, none of which differed much from the original version, and all powered by the 65hp Continental four-cylinder, horizontally-opposed, air-cooled O-170 engine.

The addition of military gear resulted in a tendency to stall and spin, which was never fully corrected. That, plus the appearance on the scene of the Piper L-4 (a pretty little J-3 Cub without its traditional yellow paint job) and the ability of Piper to build them at a rate of more than one per hour and at a price not much above the pre-war civilian price of about $1,000, carried the day.

The Aeronca was restricted to domestic operations, though a few managed to find their way to French forces in North Africa. Otherwise, most of the 1,440 built and 25 impressed were used as pre-primary trainers.

Specifications

Length: 21ft 10in
Wingspan: 35ft 0in
Height: 9ft 1in
Wing area: 169 sq ft
Empty weight: 835lb

Piper L-4/NE-1 (Cub) Grasshopper

The Piper Cub and the Douglas DC-3 were among America's greatest contributions to aviation. The DC-3 enabled airlines to show a profit and thus grow, while the Cub was used to teach more people to fly than any other airplane. In military uniform, the Cub achieved in the air what the ubiquitous Jeep did on the ground; it could go anywhere, under any conditions.

The most distant ancestor of the Cub was the 1930 Taylor E-2, arguably the first true light airplane. After more than 1,000 J-2s were built, the J-3, with improved streamlining and a fully enclosed cabin, replaced it on the assembly line. The original 50hp 3-cylinder radial Lenape engine was replaced by a 65hp Continental 4-cylinder, horizontally-opposed engine.

Maximum speed: 87mph
Maximum range: 218 miles
Service ceiling: 10,000ft

Some Surviving Examples

USAAF 42-36200 – National Museum of the U.S. Air Force
Kalamazoo Air Zoo. Michigan

L-3B
Museum of Flight, Seattle

It was this model that so impressed the colonels and generals that they ordered them by the thousands for the university-connected Civilian Pilot Training Program, first as the O-59 and then as the L-4. By the time the successor to the CPTP wound down, more than 300,000 future U.S. Army Air Forces and Navy pilots had progressed to their solo flights and beyond in Cubs.

Almost from the start, L-4As had their windows extended far enough aft to permit 360° visibility. The L-4B was the same, aside from the lack of military radios. The L-4C and L-4D were civilian airplanes impressed by the military, with two of them briefly called UC-83A. Regardless of designations, colors and military markings, they all remained unquestionably Piper Cubs.

The next three suffix letters were given, oddly enough, to other models of Piper airplanes: L-4E was for the J-4 Cub Coupe with a 75hp engine; L-4F was for the J-5 Cruiser with a 75hp engine, and L-4G was for the Cruiser with a 100hp engine. The Army returned to the J-3 Cub for the L-4H and L-4J, with a total of more than 5,500 being delivered to the Army and 250 NE-1 and NE-2 to the U.S. Navy.

It isn't known how many Cubs were used to give elementary training to pilot applicants, and how many were shipped overseas to perform a wide variety of military duties, from transporting single important passengers to spotting for the artillery, to delivering mail to the front lines and carrying wounded GIs back for emergency care.

Specifications

Length: 22ft 5in
Wingspan: 35ft 3in
Height: 6ft 8in

Wing area: 179 sq ft
Empty weight: 765lb
Maximum speed: 87mph
Maximum range: 220 miles
Service ceiling: 11,500 ft
Rate of climb: 450ft/min

Surviving Examples

L-4
Civil N42050 – National Museum of the U.S. Air Force
USAAF 44-80173 – Imperial War Museum, Duxford
Planes of Fame

L-4A
Polish Air & Space Museum
USAAF 42-36446 – National Museum of the U.S. Air Force
USAAF 42-36790 – National Museum of the U.S. Air Force

L-4B
USAAF 43-1074 – U.S. National Air & Space Museum

L-4J
USAAF 43-30426 – Valiant Air Command Warbird Museum, Titusville, Florida

Stinson L-5/OY-1 Sentinel

It was about the same size as the L-3 and L-4, but with considerably more power from its six-cylinder, horizontally-opposed 185hp Lycoming O-435 engine, it could lift more of a load from just as

short airstrips. It was the second most heavily produced American liaison airplane, with a total of almost 4,000 completed during the war.

The civilian Model 105 Voyager was the starting point, built by the Stinson Division of Consolidated Vultee, the busy manufacturer of the PBY Catalina and B-24 Liberator. As the O-62, 275 were ordered in 1942 for the primary purpose of observation, along with liaison and spotting for the Army's artillery.

The main version – the L-5 – saw 1,538 built, including 79 for the U.S. Navy and Marine Corps called the OY-1. These were followed by the next-most common type, the L-5B, which had the versatility to serve as ambulance airplanes and even as floatplanes. Of the

"Bs", 629 were for the Army, 40 were OY-1s and 60 went to the RAF as the Sentinel I.

Two hundred of the L-5C variant carried reconnaissance cameras, while the 750 L-5Es were a special Short Take-Off and Landing (STOL) version, thanks to their ailerons which drooped to add to the flap area, and to larger brakes for use on the shortest of landing strips. The final L-5E had controllable-pitch propellers; of 900 ordered, only 115 had been delivered when the war ended.

In addition to its use in all theaters of war through 1945, the L-5 served in combat during the Korean Conflict, beginning in 1950. Others were used by the quasi-governmental Civil Air Patrol for search and rescue flights well into the 1950s.

Specifications

Length: 24ft 1in
Wingspan: 34ft 0in
Height: 7ft 11in
Wing area: 155 sq ft
Empty weight: 12,550lb
Maximum speed: 163mph
Maximum range: 430 miles
Service ceiling: 15,800ft

Surviving Examples

L-5

USAAF 42-29233 – Polish Air Museum
USAAF 42-14798 – U.S. National Air & Space Museum
USAAF 42-98667 – National Museum of the U.S. Air Force
El Toro Marine Corps Base, California

L-5B

USAAF 44-16907 – Pima Air and Space Museum

L-5E

Fighter Factory,
Civil N9658H – Experimental Aircraft Association Museum

L-5G

USAAF 42-20491 – Royal Thai Air Force Museum, Bangkok

OY-1

USNM
BuAer 63085 – March Field Air Museum, California

Interstate L-6 Cadet

The first liaison airplane to be procured by the U.S. Army was built by the Interstate Aircraft & Engineering Corp., established in 1937 to build a civil light plane, the Cadet. More than 300 were manufactured between 1940 and 1942 with engines being up-graded from the original 50hp Continental A-50 to the 100hp Franklin 4ACG-199, both of them four-cylinder, horizontally-opposed powerplants.

While the Cadet out-performed its rival liaison types from Piper, Aeronca and Taylorcraft, it was more than twice as expensive and thus failed to stir much interest when the military came to ordering large quantities.

In 1942, the U.S. Army Air Forces ordered a militarized model S-1B1 as its L-6A with a 90hp Franklin engine. 250 were delivered in 1943 for the usual liaison jobs, including scouting and training. An additional eight airplanes with the Continental A-65 were delivered to the air force of Bolivia as the L-8A.

Midway through the war, Interstate became involved in developing radio-controlled powered bombs for both the Army and Navy. More than 100 were built, and many saw action, with limited success.

In 1945, all production rights to the Cadet were sold to Harlow and eventually a development was placed in production by another firm as the Arctic Tern. Interstate Aircraft & Engineering ceased to exist after a brief life.

Specifications

Length: 28ft 6in
Wingspan: 35ft 6in
Height: 7ft 0in

Wing area: 174 sq ft
Maximum weight: 1,775lb
Maximum speed: 114mph
Maximum range: 380 miles
Service ceiling: 16,500ft

Surviving Examples

S.1A
Norwegian Armed Forces Aircraft Collection, Gardermoen

Great Britain

Westland Lysander

The "Lizzie" was one of the truly versatile aircraft of World War II, thanks to considerable input into its design from active pilots. With exceptional speed range, low-speed handling characteristics and above average visibility for its pilots, the Lysander belied its obsolete appearance as it hopped into and out of tiny fields while ferrying Commandos into occupied Europe and rescuing air crew who had been shot down and managed to evade capture.

The Lysander was in the works even before the airplane it was supposed to replace had begun its service as a British Army co-operation airplane. The Hawker Hector, with its open cockpits, two wings and fixed landing gear, was intended for reconnaissance, supporting the troops and similar functions requiring an airplane with limited performance but high reliability. Just why it was fitted with a somewhat radical 24-cylinder H-style Napier Dagger engine is not clear.

As efforts to support the French underground increased, the Lysander assumed the role for which it is best known. Landing in small clearings in France at night with minimal lights for guidance, they unloaded supplies and highly trained agents, and then picked up other agents and often downed British and American flyers who had been dodging the German occupiers. They were on the ground for just a couple of minutes before staggering off at minimum flying speed and heading back to the east of England with their precious cargo.

Total production was 1,650, including 225 built in Canada mainly for training, but also for coastal patrol.

Specifications

Length: 30ft 6in
Wingspan: 50ft 0in
Height: 14ft 6in
Wing area: 260 sq ft
Empty weight: 4,365lb
Maximum speed: 212mph
Maximum range: 600 miles
Service ceiling: 21,500ft
Rate of climb: 1,250ft/min

Surviving Examples

Mk.III
RAF R9003 – Canadian Air & Space Museum
RAF R9125 – RAF Museum Hendon
RAF V9300 as "V9673" – Imperial War Museum, Duxford
RCAF 2361 – Canadian Warplane Heritage, Hamilton, Ontario

Thanks to its much lower wing-loading, the Hector could climb faster, but the Lysander could take off and land in less space and could carry a heavier load of offensive weapons. Just a year and a half after Hectors first joined active squadrons, the first Lysanders began to replace them. Shortly before the war started, most Hectors had been replaced.

At first, Lysanders were flown on missions involving dropping messages to ground forces and spotting for the artillery. Once the war began, they were sent to France and, after the Germans invaded in May 1940, they became light bombers as well, though their vulnerability to interception was so great they were soon limited to dropping supplies to the out-manned and out-gunned French and British forces.

Mk.IIIa

RCAF 2346 – U.S. National Air & Space Museum

RCAF V9312 – Imperial War Museum, Duxford

RAF V9415 – Indian Air Force Museum, New Delhi

RAF V9552 – Shuttleworth Collection, Old Warden Aerodrome

Taylorcraft Plus D/Auster 1-AOP V

The first true liaison airplane supplied to the Royal Air Force came from the same stock as the U.S. Army's Taylorcraft L-2 Grasshopper. As early as the late 1930s, the Taylorcraft Auster was a modified American light plane built on license, along with its 55hp Lycoming flat-four engine, as the Taylorcraft Plus C.

At the start of the war, 14 were impressed as the Auster I with additional visibility provided by more windows along the sides of the cockpit and across the top, aft of the wings. In July 1941, the factory began producing a more completely militarized version called the Auster I whose original engine was replaced by a 90hp straight-four Cirrus. Field trials led to an order for 100 which were the first RAF type to be called Aerial Observation Posts, or A.O.P., and were operated primarily as artillery spotters.

In 1942, the Auster III was to have been powered by the 130hp Lycoming O-290, but it was not available in sufficient numbers and so most of the 465 built used the 130hp Gypsy Major I. Not until late 1943 was the Auster III ordered and 255 of them used the Lycoming engine. They were followed by the three-seat Auster IV.

The final wartime version of the Auster was the V, equipped with additional instruments to permit flying in limited visibility weather. Some of these were used for standard liaison duties, as well as A.O.P.

In 1942, when Allied forces invaded North Africa, the Auster received its baptism under fire. They performed well in the fighting that spread to Libya, then Sicily and finally Italy. Other units were used to support the ground forces in France after D-Day.

Like its sister airplanes from Piper and Aeronca, the Auster could fly out of, and into minimum-length, rough strips immediately behind the front lines. In all, more than 1,600 Auster I through V had been built by war's end. Further versions included the A.O.P. 6 and A.O.P.9, the final model remaining in RAF service until 1957 and with the Army Air Corps until 1961.

Specifications

Length: 22ft 5in
Wingspan: 36ft 0in
Height: 8ft 0in
Wing area: 167 sq ft
Empty weight: 1,100lb
Maximum speed: 130mph
Maximum range: 250 miles

Surviving Examples

Taylorcraft Auster I
RAF LB264 – RAF Museum Hendon

Auster AOP V
RAF TJ569 – Army Air Corps Museum, RAF Middle Wallop

dH.87 Hornet Moth

DeHavilland's dH.82 Tiger Moth was an immediate success with private owners and later with the RAF as a trainer. Along with its predecessor, the dH.60 Gypsy Moth, it is credited with starting the era of the privately-owned light plane in Great Britain. DeHavilland, flush with success, followed these two with the 1934 launch of the Hornet Moth, which offered side-by-side seating.

The RAF, however, rejected it for training use, even though military airplanes were moving away from tandem seating. Beginning in 1934 with the first flight of the prototype, the manufacturer installed wings of greater taper and soon realized it had invited tip stall and difficult landing characteristics. After about 60 dH.87As had been built, deHavilland returned to the straight, unstaggered wings for the remainder of the production run of 165 Hornet Moths. Among the features which were meant to appeal to the English pilot were the folding wings and thus the greater ease and lowered cost of hangarage.

When the war began, private flying ended, which fitted in well with the government's program to take possession of any privately owned airplanes it felt were needed for the war effort. Many of the 84 Hornet Moths on the civil register in September 1939 soon found themselves wearing war paint and being flown by strangers. Most of the dH.87s were assigned to liaison units.

Specifications

Length: 25ft 0in
Wingspan: 31ft 11in
Height: 6ft 7in
Wing area: 245 sq ft
Empty weight: 1,240lb

The British Army needed a versatile, reliable airplane that could fly slowly and serve as an aerial observation post, spotting for the artillery. The prototype, which flew in September 1942, was a modified M.28 Mercury, a potentially useful design for which the manufacturer did not have the needed production capacity.

While the Messenger might have filled the need for which it was intended, only 23 examples of the Messenger 1 were built for the RAF. Along with being flown as liaison airplanes, they were used as VIP transports and gained fame as the personal airplanes of top military men such as Field Marshal Sir Bernard "Monty" Montgomery.

When the war ended, 19 of the original 23 had survived and were sold to private owners as the Messenger 4A. The type 2A, with a 150hp Blackburn Cirrus Major 3 replacing the 130hp deHavilland Gypsy Major ID, entered production, with 65 eventually built, of a total of just 93.

Maximum speed: 124mph
Maximum range: 620 miles
Service ceiling: 14,800 ft
Rate of climb: 690ft/min

Surviving Examples

Civil G-ADOT – deHavilland Heritage Museum

Miles Messenger
While most Allied World War II liaison airplanes started off as light private airplanes which were then militarized, the Messenger began in answer to a military requirement and then donned civil garb.

Specifications

Length: 24ft 0in
Wingspan: 36ft 2in
Height: 7ft 6in
Wing area: 191 sq ft
Empty weight: 1,450lb
Maximum speed: 135mph
Service ceiling: 16,000ft
Rate of climb: 950ft/min

Surviving Examples

Mk.2A
Civil G-AJOC – Ulster Folk & Transport Museum, County Down,
 Northern Ireland

Miles M.3 Falcon

In the 1930s, Miles Aircraft, Ltd. developed a reputation for clean, sporty airplanes that extracted considerable speed from limited horsepower, such as the Hawk Speed Six and the Sparrowhawk. The three-seat prototype of the M.3 first flew in October 1934 with a 130hp deHavilland Gypsy engine. It wasn't long before the four-seat version – M.3A Falcon Major – was in production, 18 being built before being superseded by the M.3B Falcon Six which reverted to three seats.

Soon, three M.3Bs were being used by the Royal Aircraft Establishment to test new wings and improved aerodynamics. The M.3C was a four-seat airplane with dual controls and a 200hp deHavilland Gypsy Six engine. The M.3D and M.3E were similar and also built in very small numbers.

When the war began, 10 Falcons were impressed into service with the Royal Air Force, Royal Navy and other militaries. Six of them were still flying at war's end and resumed their civilian identities.

Specifications

Length: 25ft 0in
Wingspan: 35ft 0in
Height: 6ft 6in
Wing area: 174 sq ft
Empty weight: 1,300lb
Maximum speed: 145mph
Maximum range: 615 miles

Service ceiling: 15,000ft
Rate of climb: 750ft/min

Surviving Examples

Civil M.3A
G-AEEG, private owner, at Old Warden Aerodrome

Percival Gull

Edgar Percival founded the Percival Aircraft Co. in 1932 and almost immediately had a success, the P.1 Gull. Lacking production facilities, he arranged for the British Aircraft Co. to build the prototype, which flew in July 1932. Unlike the open-cockpit biplanes which were common at the time, his Gull was a cantilever, low-wing monoplane that carried a pilot and two passengers in a completely enclosed cabin.

With speed and range that exceeded its rivals, the Gull went into production by Parnall Aircraft, which built 24 of them, called the Gull Four and powered by a mixture of 130hp Cirrus and Gypsy Major, and 160hp Napier Javelin engines. They were some of the earliest business transports, but gained fame for a series of speed and distance flights. After the first batch, all future Gulls were built in Percival's new factory.

The final version was the Gull Six, being a model Four with a 200hp deHavilland Gypsy Six engine and modified canopy and landing gear. This airplane led to the Vega Gull.

Its military service was limited, consisting of a half dozen Gull Sixes impressed into the RAF and Royal Navy. The excellent performance of the Six led the military to order a version of the Vega Gull known as the Percival Proctor.

Specifications

Length: 24ft 9in
Wingspan: 36ft 2in
Height: 7ft 5in
Wing area: 169 sq ft
Empty weight: 1,170lb
Maximum speed: 145mph
Maximum range: 700 miles
Service ceiling: 16,000ft
Rate of climb: 850ft/min

Surviving Examples

P.1
G-ACGR (prototype) – Brussels Air Museum

Vega Gull
c/n K305 – civil ZK-DPP in New Zealand
civil G-AECJ – Little Gransden

Germany

Fieseler Fi.156 Storch ("Stork")

A strong case can be made for the Storch being the world's first purpose-built Short Take-Off and Landing (STOL) airplane. When it was still against the Treaty of Versailles for Germany to build military airplanes, the prototype exhibited exceptional short-field performance with a take-off in as little as 100 feet and landing in less than 200.

Such performance was achieved by a wing-loading almost as low as a Piper Cub, plenty of power (from its 240hp Argus V-8) for an airplane of its size, along with full-span slotted flaps and a fixed leading-edge flap. Top speed and rate-of-climb were reduced, but it was a profitable trade-off. For convenience of storage and transport by land, the wings could be folded back alongside the fuselage.

The prototype flew in May, 1936, with production of the first small batch beginning in the summer of 1937. While a few Fi.156Bs were built, the Fieseler factory didn't get into large-scale production until the introduction of the Fi.156C in late 1937. Through the end of the war in 1945, some 1,900 were built in Germany, with almost 800 by

Morane-Saulnier in occupied France and 1,250 more in occupied Czechoslovakia. This "licensed" production filled the demand when the need for fighters occupied all available manufacturing facilities.

Once France was liberated in 1944, the reconstituted French aircraft industry included the building of the Morane-Saulnier M.S. 500 version of the Storch. The first ones used left-over German engines, and when the supply ran out they were replaced by radial engines, including the 230hp Salmson, the 300hp Jacobs and finally the 235hp Lycoming.

A wide variety of versions were built, as well as others that were tested but never produced. The Fi.156C appeared as a liaison and observation airplane, some fitted with skis and others with filters for tropical operations. The Fi.156D was an ambulance airplane

with a large cabin and loading doors. Limited numbers were built of the "E", with small tank treads for rough-field landings, and the "F" as a counter-insurgency version with machine guns and racks for small bombs or smoke generators. The last was the Fi.156U anti-submarine model which could carry a single depth charge.

Post-war production consisted of the M.S.500 through 505 in France and the Mráz K-65 in Czechoslovakia. In all, more than 3,000 Storches were built.

Specifications

Length: 32ft 6in
Wingspan: 46ft 9in
Height: 10ft 0in
Wing area: 280 sq ft
Empty weight: 1,990lb
Maximum speed: 110mph
Maximum range: 240 miles
Service ceiling: 15,100ft
Rate of climb: 950ft/min

Surviving Examples

Fi.156
Luftwaffe 080138 – U.S. National Air & Space Museum

Fi.156C
RAF VP746 – Royal Air Force Museum, Cosford
s/n 4362 – Flying Heritage Collection
s/n 4389 – National Museum of the U.S. Air Force
Luftwaffe 475081, RR+KE – RAF Museum, Cosford
Deutsches Technik
Yugoslav Air Museum

Focke Wulf FW.58 Weihe ("Kite")

The primary purpose of this light twin was as an advanced Luftwaffe trainer for radio operators, aerial gunners and pilots. The prototype FW.58V-1 flew in the summer of 1935 and the major production version began delivery within a few months. It was mixture of new and old ideas, with the pilot and co-pilot having a fully enclosed canopy, while the wing was supported by a strut from the rear of the engine cowl to the side of the fuselage.

In addition to serving in the training role, the Weihe was used as a VIP transport, short-haul airliner by Lufthansa, air ambulance, for aerial surveying and for weather reconnaissance. As a light bomber, it had a single .30 cal. machine gun firing from a permanently open section behind the cockpit and another in the glazed nose. Bomb load consisted of several 55lb bombs.

Power was from a pair of 240hp inverted inline Argus AC-10 engines. Total production approached 2,000, with more than 300 exported to many European countries under German control, along with Sweden, China and Argentina. More than 25 were built under license in Brazil.

Specifications (sources vary considerably)

Length: 45ft 11in
Wingspan: 68ft 11in
Height: 12ft 9in or 14ft 1in
Wing area: 506 sq ft
Empty weight: 4,200–5,290lb
Maximum speed: 159–174mph
Maximum range: 500 miles
Service ceiling: 18,370ft
Rate of climb: 950ft/min

Surviving Example

FW-58B-2
AT-Fw-1530 – Aerospace Museum, Rio de Janiero, Brazil

Japan

Tachikawa Ki.36 Ida

It was a typical 1930s Japanese Army cooperation or liaison airplane, with good maneuverability but only moderate speed and range. The prototype, with a 450hp Kitachi radial engine, first flew in April 1938 and was chosen over the rival Mitsubishi

The final use of the remaining Ki.36s was the same as for so many obsolete Japanese airplanes of various categories. With quickly affixed 1,100-lb. bombs, they became kamikaze weapons, ending their days in attacks on Allied warships. A development with a more powerful engine and retractable landing gear never got into production.

Specifications

Length: 25ft 3in
Wingspan: 38ft 9in
Height: 11ft 11in
Wing area: 215 sq ft
Empty weight: 2,750lb
Maximum speed: 215mph
Maximum range: 770 miles
Service ceiling: 26,750ft
Rate of climb: 1,480ft/min

Surviving Examples

Royal Thai Air Force Museum, Bangkok
People's Liberation Army Air Force Museum, Beijing

Ki.35 for production, which began the following November and continued until January 1944, by which time more than 1,300 had been manufactured.

It saw its first combat against the Chinese, whose fighters were decidedly second rate. Later, when the British and Americans entered the Pacific war, their more modern, high-performance fighters revealed the Ki.36's sub-standard speed and other basic weaknesses. The Ki-36s were quickly recalled to the fighting on the Chinese mainland, where their good handling and reliability pointed toward their use as an advanced trainer. With modifications, the Ki.36 became the Ki.55.

Chapter 5

Gliders

The first man-carrying, heavier-than-air flying machines were gliders built by the likes of Otto Lilienthal in Germany, Percy Pilcher in Great Britain and the Wright brothers in the U.S.A. Rather than being an end in themselves, they were a stepping stone toward man's greater goal of powered flight. All three pioneers planned to add small engines as soon as they had learned enough from brief glides. Once gliders had progressed to airplanes, they ceased to be a major concern of the aeronautical community, re-emerging years later as sporting aircraft. With ever-longer and more efficient wings, what had become sailplanes carried their pilots on flights of greater distance, height and duration.

Military uses for gliders date back to the early 1920s when, in secret, the U.S.S.R. and what would soon become Nazi Germany used a loophole in the Treaty of Versailles to operate schools in the U.S.S.R. to train Germans to fly gliders in preparation for flying military airplanes, something that was prevented by the Treaty.

As the Luftwaffe's glider program became known, Britain and the U.S.A. instituted their own schemes to train pilots to fly future troop- and equipment-carrying gliders that would slip silently into enemy territory in surprise attacks. Simple two-seat training gliders were quickly created from existing civil models, while larger ones were being developed for operational use. After World War II, military gliders rapidly faded out of use.

United States of America

Frankfort TG-1 "Cinema"

Manufacture of the civil Cinema I began in 1938, but demand soon forced its replacement by the Cinema II high-performance two-seat training sailplane. In 1941, when the U.S. Army Air Corps decided it needed small gliders to train pilots to fly much larger combat gliders, it signed developmental contracts with four companies that had reputations for designing and building gliders. Frankfort was the first to become involved, offering a mildly modified version of its Cinema II as the TG-1A.

In 1942, 42 were produced, unfortunately late and lacking the required structural strength and flying characteristics for use by hurriedly recruited soldiers, most of whom had little or no prior flying experience. Eventually, a few Cinema IIs were purchased from their civilian owners and became TG-1B through to D, but Frankfort's part in what was becoming a major manufacturing program came to a premature end.

Specifications of the Cinema II

Length: 23ft 4in
Wingspan: 44ft 3in
Empty weight: 500lb
Glide ratio: 20:1

The TG-2 was built from strategic materials – steel and aluminum – and so a wooden version was drawn up and became the TG-3A, of which 114 were delivered. By this time, the U.S. Army Air Forces had decided its need would be better filled by modified liaison airplanes from Aeronca, Taylorcraft and Piper, which, in turn, were militarized civilian light planes.

Specifications

Length: 25ft 0in
Wingspan: 52ft 0in
Height: 8ft 0in
Wing area: 214 sq ft
Empty weight: 450lb
Glide ratio: 23: 1

Surviving Example

Civil N53601 – U.S. National Air & Space Museum

Schweizer TG-2/TG-3/LNS-1

The three teenaged Schweizer brothers built their first flying machine – a primary glider – in 1930 then taught themselves to fly in their own handiwork. By the time the U.S. Army Air Corps recognized its need for training gliders in 1941, the Schweizer Aircraft Corp. had its two-place commercial Model 2-8 ready for a coat of olive drab paint. In 1942, they delivered 32, while 7 more were purchased from their private owners.

Laister-Kaufman TG-4A

The TG-4 was the last of a series of quickly prepared designs meant to train Army and Navy glider pilots. But, being slightly modified sailplanes flown by civilian soaring instructors, they were actually being used to teach their unsuspecting (but no doubt pleased) students the joys of soaring, in which the goals are the achieving of ever-greater distances and altitude by using invisible columns of rising warm air (thermals).

Such skills, while of great importance to sporting pilots, are of no consequence to those whose futures would involve long, nerve-wracking towed flights, followed by quick, silent dashes to the ground, all too often while facing enemy fire. Once the military brass worked out what was going on, they turned to light plane manufacturers who realized that what were needed were engineless, rebalanced Aeroncas, Taylorcraft and Pipers.

Surviving Examples

TG-2
Civil N54301 – March Field Air Museum, California

LNS-1
U.S. Marine Corps Air Museum, Quantico, Virginia
U.S. National Museum of Naval Aviation
BuAer 04383 – Kalamazoo Air Zoo, Michigan

TG-3A
USAAF 42-52958 – National Museum of the U.S. Air Force
USAAF 42-52983 – Imperial War Museum, Duxford

Specifications

Length: 21ft 3in
Wingspan: 50ft 0in
Height: 4ft 0in
Wing area: 166 sq ft
Empty weight: 475lb
Glide ratio: 22:1

Surviving Examples

N53612 – Planes of Fame
USAAF 42-43734 –National Museum of the U.S. Air Force

Taylorcraft TG-6

Start with a factory-fresh Taylorcraft L-2 liaison airplane, remove the engine, extend the nose to allow space for a flight instructor, extend the canopy all the way to the nose and you have a training glider. Then all you have to do is to beef up some of the structure to resist some unusual stresses expected when novice pilots have yet to learn to move the flight controls smoothly.

The first of the TG-2s was modified from an L-2 in just over a week, as the rag-and-tube construction was highly amenable to rapid changes, unlike that of more sophisticated and higher performance airplanes. Series production went quickly as well, with 250 gliders being delivered in a few months.

Since operational flights of combat gliders were expected to be very short in duration and low in altitude, their trainers could be almost as simple. An airplane's engine instruments were not needed, nor were navigational instruments, which would be in the tow plane. There was no need for either an electrical system or fuel tanks.

Many hundreds of enlisted men learned to fly these simple craft without ever having flown powered airplanes. Their operational flights would be measured in minutes, and so they received no more training than was absolutely necessary. For practical advanced training, the student pilots then moved on to Waco CG-4A cargo gliders, which they would eventually fly in action. When the war was ending, the surviving TG-6 gliders were sold as surplus, with many of them being re-converted into Taylorcraft light planes.

Specifications

Length: 23ft 0in
Wingspan: 35ft 5in
Height: 7ft 11in
Wing area: 181 sq ft
Gross weight: 1,260lb

Surviving Example

USAAF 42-58662 – Pima Air and Space Museum

Pratt Read TG-32/LNE-1

In the late 1930s the U.S. Navy contemplated using gliders in what was becoming an inevitable war in the Pacific. For the training of its glider pilots, it contracted with Pratt, Read & Co. for a two-seat (for student and instructor) monoplane having a steel tube fuselage covered with fabric, along with wings and tail entirely of wood: the LNE-1.

The XLNE-1 flew in 1940 and led to an order for 100 gliders, which were delivered to the Navy, which thereupon decided against using gliders in any foreseeable aspect of the Pacific war. Seventy-three of them were transferred to the Army Air Force as TG-32s and were promptly put into storage, where they remained until sold as surplus at the end of the war. Like the other training gliders, they never went overseas.

Specifications

Length: 26ft 3in
Wingspan: 54ft 6in
Height: 6ft
Wing area: 230 sq ft
Empty weight: 585lb

Surviving Example

BuAer 31521 – flying, Lovettsville, VA

Waco CG-4A Hadrian

While the U.S. Army Air Corps struggled to find just what it needed to train glider pilots, when it came to an operational troop- and cargo-carrier, the decision was made and was never changed, as the Army turned to a small firm known best for its sporty open-cockpit biplanes. The Waco CG-4A was built in numbers exceeded only by a few types of fighters and bombers: 13,900. Some of the 16 companies that turned out complete aircraft were as well known as the Ford Motor Co. and Cessna Aircraft; others were considerably less so, such as Wick and Robertson and the Ward Furniture Co. Most of them operated three 8-hour shifts per day in expectation of a major glider war.

The prototype of the CG-4 flew in May 1942, and by August, Whiteman Field (now the home of the Northrop B-2 stealth bomber) was being prepared to welcome the first of the big gliders and their C-46 and C-47 tow-planes, along with those who would fly them. Known then as Sedalia Army Air Field, it was also the site for training parachute troops.

The CG-4A had the capacity to carry 13 fully equipped soldiers, or a Jeep, or a 75 mm howitzer, or a ¼-ton trailer, all loaded and unloaded through the nose section which hinged upward like on the much later Lockheed C-5A. Just how great were the emergency overloads has not been recorded, though the urgency of glider operations suggests they were considerable.

The first operation to use large numbers of the Waco gliders was the July 1943 invasion of Sicily, the first step on the road to the liberation of Italy. They achieved their greatest fame during the D-Day invasion of France's Normandy coast, though many of the gliders were lost due to planning and navigational errors. Nevertheless, they continued to be used, though in smaller numbers, in both the European and even Pacific theaters of war.

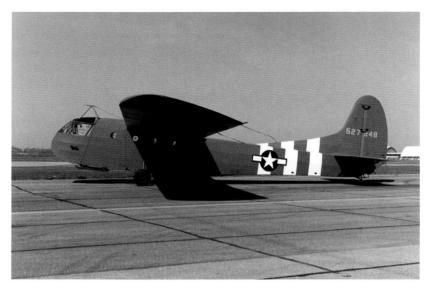

Specifications

Length: 48ft8in
Wingspan: 83ft 8in
Height: 15ft 4in
Wing area: 900 sq ft
Empty weight: 3,900lb

Surviving Examples

USAAF 45-27948 – National Museum of the U.S. Air Force
Cradle of Aviation Museum
USAAF unknown – Kalamazoo Air Zoo, Michigan
Airborne D-Day Museum, St. Mere Eglise, France

A serious effort was made to develop a powered version of the CG-4 under the "PG" (for powered glider) designation. Several were modified with pairs of engines ranging from the 125hp Franklin horizontally-opposed six through the 200hp Ranger inline six in hopes that they might be able to fly their way out of trouble. While 10 PG-2A's were built, the idea never was a success.

The final development was the CG-15A, a slightly up-dated version, which would have replaced the CG-4A, had there been a need. One of the prototypes became the PG-3 with the addition of two 225hp Jacobs radial engines. Two others were tested by the U.S. Navy as the XLR2W-1. More than 400 CG-15A's were built, and the remainder of the 1,000 ordered was canceled at the end of the war.

Great Britain

Airspeed Horsa

It was the success of the Germans' use of gliders in the battles for France and Belgium in 1940 that convinced the RAF and USAAF to rush development of similar aircraft for use in airborne operations. By late 1940, the British had flown the prototype of the General Aircraft Hotspur, intended to land troops behind enemy lines. Lacking the capacity needed for operations then foreseen, it was soon relegated to training duties, which it fulfilled well. The only Hotspur, on view at the Museum of Army Flying, is a reproduction.

In late June, 1940, Prime Minister Winston Churchill initiated a study of the need for a 5,000-man parachute force. While this was being created, it was expanded to include a large number of gliders to land armed troops, as well as men to operate equipment that had been dropped into battle. A large glider that could carry as many as 30 fully-armed soldiers or objects as weighty as light tanks was ordered in February 1941 and emerged in prototype form in September as the Horsa.

An early plan to turn the Horsa into some sort of gliding bomb, with up to 4,000lb of high explosive in the fuselage, was dropped when the production of more conventional bombers accelerated.

By May 1942 more than 2,300 Horsas had been ordered, with components to be built by small wood shops and furniture makers, and assembled by RAF Maintenance Units under the watchful eye of Airspeed, once the initial order of almost 700 had been built. Total production of the Horsa was between 3,800 and 5,000 depending on the source of data.

The fuselage was built in three sections that were then bolted together. The door for loading freight was on the left side and could be lowered to permit ground-level access. For rapid unloading, the aft section could be broken away at the joint. In later versions, the nose could be swung aside so that small vehicles could be driven on and off. In addition, as many as three small cargo containers could be attached under the in-board section of either wing.

The first combat use of the Horsa was in November 1942 for an unsuccessful attack on a German heavy-water plant in Norway, which was part of the Reich's effort to develop nuclear weapons. Next, 30 Horsas were towed to North Africa by Handley Page Halifax heavy bombers, with the surviving 27 being used in the July 1943 invasion of Sicily.

As many as 600 of the big gliders took part in the invasion of Normandy, including the landing of more than 100 soldiers to capture a vital bridge over the Caen Canal. In Operation Market Garden, more than 1,200 Horsas were towed into action by hundreds of Douglas C-47 transports and Short Stirling bombers.

Some 400 Horsas were transferred to the U.S. Army Air Forces, as no American-built gliders could carry the required loads.

Specifications

Length: 67ft 0in
Wingspan: 88ft 0in
Height: 19ft 6in
Wing area: 1,104 sq ft
Empty weight: 8,370lb

Surviving Example

RAF KJ351 – The Museum of Army Flying, Middle Wallop

General Aircraft Hamilcar

It was as big as a Lancaster bomber and could have played a major role in Allied offensive operations, had there not been serious deficiencies in the administration of the program and the manufacturer's ability to produce this large aircraft on schedule. When it finally got into action, the lack of realistic tests and training combined to reduce its ability to meet the difficult challenges facing any aircraft lacking its own source of propulsion.

It was clear from the start of British interest in combat gliders that a primary need was for a cargo-carrier that could airlift several tons of equipment and supplies –including light tanks – to and beyond the front lines of battle with a minimum of losses to men and materiel. The Hamilcar was to be that vehicle.

In early 1941 the basic design was settled: an all-wood airframe with the capability of lifting as much as 17,000lb, including a tank or two transport vehicles or a medium-size field artillery piece, along with ammunition and men to operate them. Plans were already well along for Allied offensive operations, including invasions of German-occupied territories.

Sadly, the inability of the manufacturer to organize production, and of the government to decide exactly what it wanted, combined to delay the completion of the first production Hamilcar for 2½ years! Gradually, the program gathered speed, and by the approach of D-Day, several dozen were ready, as were their crews.

They headed off for Normandy with vitally needed men and equipment, and promptly encountered a series of setbacks, at least a few of which should have been predicted and dealt with in advance. Some suffered broken tow ropes; others had to turn back when the over-stressed engines of their tow plane lost power. One crashed on the way when its tank broke loose and smashed into the cockpit. Of those which got near the drop zones, some ran into other gliders and into their own tanks on the ground, while German gunners shot down several of the large, slow, cumbersome craft.

Poor planning and execution prevented the Hamilcar from being a major element in the liberation of western Europe. The total production of fewer than 400 was not sufficient for its planned operations.

Specifications

Length: 68ft 0in
Wingspan: 110ft 0in
Height: 20ft 3in
Wing area: 1,658 sq ft
Empty weight: 18,400lb
Gross weight: 36,000lb

Surviving Example

Partial restoration – The Museum of Army Flying, Middle Wallop

Germany

DFS 108-14

A 21st Century glider or sailplane features the very latest in aerodynamic and structural design, and can soar for many hours and for hundreds of miles after being towed aloft. In contrast, the earliest gliders, which preceded powered airplanes by a few years, were exceedingly simple, those of Otto Lilienthal and Octave Chanute having no fuselages, and landing gear consisting of the pilot's legs and feet. Today they would be called hang-gliders.

Following on those elemental craft were the primary gliders, which had fuselages no more than a few inches wide, no enclosure for the pilot, and only a skid for landing. Not capable of true soaring, they nevertheless provided enough time in the sky to appeal to hundreds of men and women who wanted to fly for as little fuss and cost as possible.

During the war, the DFS 108-14 was used to give students their first taste of motorless flight, including the feel of wind in the pilot's face. After the war, many of these primary gliders found their way into private hands.

Surviving Example

USAAF FE-5004? – U.S. National Air & Space Museum

DFS.230

The highly successful Nazi attack on the Belgian fort of Eban-Emael in May 1940 saw the first use of a new type of aircraft, the assault glider. Thanks to the glider's near-total silence (and to the failure of the Germans to declare war on Belgium), the large defensive garrison was overcome by glider-borne troops landing on its roof, which was the only undefended area.

Such use of specially designed and equipped gliders in an attack behind enemy lines was quickly studied by the top men in the American and British air forces that would soon be facing the Germans in a new phase of the war assumed to be in the very near future. In hopes of making up for lost time, plans were made to develop their first military gliders for a variety of purposes.

By the time the DFS.230 was in development, Germany's wholesale disregard for the "no military aircraft" provisions of the Treaty of Versailles had become common knowledge. Because of the planned use of the assault glider, its testing and production were kept secret to prevent defenses from being built. The first one flew in late 1937, with production not starting until October 1939 due to a lack of enthusiasm among some highly placed officials.

The first use of this, or any other assault glider, was in the capture of the Belgian fort by a much smaller force of German airborne soldiers. Ten 230s, carrying 78 troops, were able to seal off the Belgians inside the fort and also capture several vital bridges until conventional forces could arrive.

There was nothing particularly novel in either the design or construction of the glider, only in its use. Typically, one could carry nine soldiers plus as much as 600lb of equipment, ammunition and other supplies. When a 230 was towed off by a tri-motored

Ju.52 transport, it used a two-wheeled dolly which could then be jettisoned, forcing it to land on a skid.

Subsequent operations in which they were used include the April 1941 invasion of Greece and the May battle for the island of Crete. In the latter, some 13,000 glider infantry soldiers and paratroops were used and suffered more than 5,000 casualties. That was the last major battle for German glider-borne troops.

The main production version was the DFS.230 A-1, followed by the B-1 which used a braking parachute and a single machine gun to be used at the time of landing. The final major type was the C-1 with braking rockets in the nose. The F-1 development would have carried double the payload, had it not been canceled.

Specifications

Length: 37ft 0in
Wingspan: 69ft 1in
Height: 9ft 4in
Wing area: 410 sq ft
Empty weight: 1,700lb
Payload: 2,730lb
Maximum glide: 18:1

Surviving Example

8-5209 AI– Ailes Anciennes, le Bourget, France

Grunau Baby IIb

Since Germany had signed the World War I peace treaty agreeing not to build military aircraft or train military pilots, it had to at least appear to be in compliance. But since revenge was on the minds of so many Germans, what was needed was a system for training pilots to fly powered aircraft without actually doing so.

Enter the single-seat training sailplane, which gave every indication of being a sporting craft and not the prototype of some later machine that could carry guns and bombs. The Grunau Baby fit perfectly, having been designed for both training and soaring on whatever thermals could be found. The first example flew in 1931 and by the next year had been redesigned to create the Baby II, which rapidly gained a reputation for its flying qualities and its sturdiness.

1932, however, was also the year in which Hitler took command of Germany and set it on the path to destruction. Hundreds of the simple machine were quickly built to give members of the official German Sport Flying Organization a chance to learn the basics of flight. That they would soon move on to powered trainers and then operational fighters and bombers was understood, if not widely publicized.

By the start of the war in September 1939, thousands of Baby II and IIb were flying daily and helping to turn out those who would fly Messerschmitts and Heinkels and Junkers that had first been built in secret and later in the open. When the Wehrmacht crashed across the Polish border without warning, Grunau graduates spread terror with their dive bombing and strafing attacks on their neighbors.

At war's end, total production of the open-cockpit glider had exceeded 4,000 and was far from over. Scores more were built in France by Nord as the Elliots Eon, in England as the Slingsby T5, in Australia by designer Edmund Schneider as the Baby 4, and in Sweden for use by the Air Force. Total production is unknown, but must have been at least 5,000.

Specifications

Length: 20ft 0in
Wingspan: 44ft 6in
Wing area: 153 sq ft
Empty weight: 375lb
Payload: 175lb
Glide ratio: 17:1

Surviving Examples

USAAF FE-2600 – U.S. National Air & Space Museum
PL-33, PL-338 – Quatro Vientos, Spain

Gotha Go.242A

The success of the Luftwaffe's DFS.230 assault glider led quickly to plans for a much larger troop and cargo glider, which was realized in the Gotha 242. It had a bulky fuselage, slender twin tail booms

and landing gear consisting of two main wheels and a long skid. One could carry as many as 23 fully equipped soldiers or up to 7,000lb of cargo or any of several combinations, depending on the situation.

The first two built – prototypes – flew in 1941, with quantity production beginning soon thereafter. Large clamshell doors opened to load and unload troops, while a hinged rear section of the fuselage swung open to load the cargo version. Since overloading was seen as a frequent problem, the basic glider was tested with four 100-lb solid-fuel rockets at the rear of the cargo hold, and with a single liquid-fuel rocket slung under each wing, both devices to be used for short-field take-offs.

Launching such a heavy craft posed problems, though most were towed off behind He.111 bombers or Ju.52 transports. Most of their

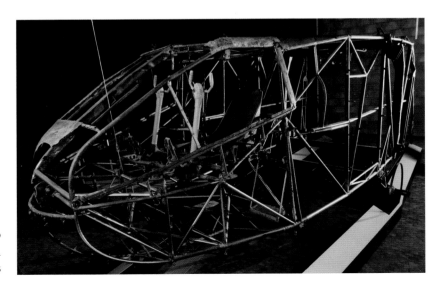

use was in the southern part of Europe, mainly North Africa, and the Mediterranean and Aegean Seas areas. There was a scheme to build a version with a boat-style hull, to be used to land near a ship and launch a small boat carrying several thousand pounds of high explosive. While several were built, none saw action.

In line with early plans, a powered version – the Go.244 – went into production as soon as 700hp Gnome-Rhone radial engines became available from a captured French factory. Forty-three were built as Go.244s, while another 133 were modified from Go.242 gliders. Total production of Gotha gliders was in excess of 1,500.

Specifications

Length: 52ft 10in
Wingspan: 80ft 5in
Height: 14ft 11in
Wing area: 672 sq ft
Empty weight: 7,055lb

Surviving Example

Deutsches Technik Museum, Berlin

Italy

CAT T.2

Some aircraft severely try the definition of having been involved in the Second World War. The TM.2, while unquestionably built and flown during the period, was destroyed on its second test flight and the project was promptly canceled. Its impact was near zero, but nevertheless earned it a place in this book.

With a very clean fuselage and a long, tapered wing fit for a sailplane, it was to have carried up to 10 fully armed soldiers or cargo up to 2,850lb as the Italian version of Germany's DFS.230 assault glider.

The first flight, under tow by a Fiat CR.42 biplane fighter, was on 22 February 1943, and was sufficiently successful for the manufacturer to schedule a second flight for the following day. That one began normally, but at an altitude of about 150 feet, the tow rope became detached from the tow plane, and the pilot of the glider was suddenly on his own with the glider's nose pointed upward. This almost certainly led to a stall and the beginning of a spin. Lacking sufficient altitude to attempt a recovery, the glider hit the ground hard and was destroyed, killing its pilot and passenger.

While a second prototype had been completed and could have been tested, the program was stopped at this point, while other glider programs continued. The second TM 2 survived the war and eventually was placed on display in the Museum of Science and Technology in Milan. It was later transferred to the Italian Air Force Museum, where at last report it was in storage.

Specifications

Length: 23ft 5in
Wingspan: 74ft 10in
Height: 15ft 6in
Wing area: 495 sq ft
Empty weight: 3,750lb
Payload: 2,865lb

Surviving Example

Italian Air Force MM511 (second prototype) – Italian Air Force Museum

Chapter 6

Rotary Wing

The race to develop the world's first heavier-than-air flying machine did not focus exclusively on fixed-wing airplanes. There were those who were convinced success would come with ornithopters, whose flapping wings most resembled those of birds. Yet others dreamed of vertical take-offs and landings with what became known as helicopters. The reasons for the great success of airplanes and the protracted lack of success of the others have been described and explained in great detail elsewhere.

While the dwindling supply of friends of the ornithopter have yet to admit defeat despite a century of disappointment, the helicopter first experienced a short period of apparent progress, then faded away while scattered experimenters toiled to solve its many and complex problems. Just who made the first vertical take-off with whirling blades may never be known, or at least agreed upon.

As early as 1907, Frenchman Paul Cornu is said to have raised his vehicle from the ground for a few seconds without outside assistance. In 1922, Henry and Emile Berliner (no relation to the author) flew an estimated distance of 200 feet while several feet above the ground. Two years later, Etienne Oehmichen flew non-stop around a one-kilometer course, averaging almost 5mph.

True success for the helicopter came only when men saw the military potential of an aircraft that could operate from almost any flat surface larger than itself.

United States of America

Platt LePage XR-1

The U.S. Army's first helicopter flew almost seven months before the U.S.A. entered World War II and even longer before the Army's first Sikorsky flew, though few knew about any of this at the time. The R-1 was also the first (and probably the last) U.S. military helicopter to have its rotors off to the sides on long outriggers.

It was the winner of a design competition over a Sikorsky helicopter and autogyro designs from Pitcairn and Kellett, The prototype XR-1 flew three months late in May, 1941, which permitted the future Sikorsky R-4 to also receive financial support. The basic idea of the XR-1 was apparently inspired by the German Focke Wulf FW.61, which LePage had seen.

Much of the XR-1 was an airplane, with a fuselage, tail and wing-like outriggers that produced some lift in forward flight. Its two large rotors were driven by a 450hp Pratt & Whitney R-985 radial, air-cooled engine which was located in the fuselage and connected to the rotors by long drive shafts.

For the first flight, the helicopter was tethered to the ground, though about six weeks later it achieved its first low-altitude free flight. As it gradually was flown higher and faster, problems were revealed, including ineffective flight controls and severe vibrations. In view of the novelty of the helicopter concept and what later would be recognized as the difficulty in developing very complex rotor hubs, this was not surprising.

The most difficult of the problems were not significantly reduced until 1943, by which time the R-4 had proven highly successful and had gone into production. Additional delays to the R-1 program resulted from its July 1943 accident which was due to no fault in the aircraft. It would not return to the air for a year.

An improved XR-1A entered the test program in the spring of 1943 with modified controls and better performance. It was flown cross-country to Wright Field, Dayton, Ohio, for additional testing, which ended when parts in the rotor hub broke. That crash landing was severe enough for Platt-LePage to sell the wreckage for scrap.

The original prototype was back in the air and the Army was sufficiently impressed to order seven pre-production aircraft.

Failure of the manufacturer to deliver these on schedule, combined with persisting problems with control and vibration, along with the much more rapid progress with Sikorsky's R-4, resulted in the entire contract being canceled in April 1945, almost five years after the program began.

Efforts to develop the R-1 into a civilian helicopter failed. The XR-1A was bought by the new Piasecki Co. and the airframe was used in an attempt to build a tilt-rotor style convertiplane, a very difficult challenge that finally was achieved some 50 years later.

Specifications

Length: 29ft 4in
Wingspan: 65ft 0in
Rotor diameter: 30ft 6in
Height: 9ft 0in
Gross weight: 4,730lb
Maximum speed: 110mph

Sole Surviving Example

XR-1
USAAC 41-001– U.S. National Air & Space Museum

Kellett R-2/O-60

Before there were helicopters (or at least helicopters that *worked*) there were autogyros. The Kellett Autogiro Co. had been building and flying these rotary-wing aircraft since the early 1930s. Its KD-1, similar to the Cierva C.30, was modified into the KD-1A, certified by the Civil Aeronautics Authority (CAA) and placed into

production on a limited scale in 1937 and used to carry the mail on an experimental basis by Eastern Airlines.

The U.S. Army acquired a KD-1 in 1935 for evaluation (calling it the XO-60), then bought seven improved versions to use as YO-60 observation aircraft. When powered by a 225 Jacobs radial engine to provide forward thrust, one of them became the YG-1B. Then with a 300hp Jacobs radial engine, the YG-1C finally became the XR-2, as the designation was changed from G for Gyro to R for Rotary-wing on the way to the eventual H for Helicopter.

During tests, which had to be much more stringent and far-ranging than for conventional airplanes, the XR-2 was wrecked on the ground by rotor resonance, one of many new problems arising when an aircraft's wing rotates at high speed. The Army continued to experiment with this new form of flying machine, approving of some of its unusual performance characteristics such as near-vertical take-offs and vertical landings, but concerned with its excessive need for maintenance.

While the Kelletts were gradually improved, they were simultaneously being shoved into the background by the newer and even more versatile helicopter. Even as the Army was learning how to use its YO-60s, Sikorsky R-4s were being shipped overseas to the fighting fronts, where they began to distinguish themselves in rescuing downed pilots, transporting seriously injured GIs to hospitals, and ferrying parts from depots to where they were needed.

The Kellett YO-60/R-2 had its brief time in the spotlight before the day of the military autogyro came to an end.

Specifications

Length: 21ft 5in
Rotor diameter: 42ft 0in
Height: 10ft 3in
Gross weight: 2,640lb
Maximum speed: 127mph
Service ceiling: 14,000ft

Surviving Example

XO-60
USAAF 42-13610 – U.S. National Air & Space Museum

Sikorsky R-4/HNS-1/Hoverfly Mk.1

Igor Sikorsky was one of several inventors who tried to invent the helicopter in the days before World War I. In Czarist Russia he came to close to flying such a craft in 1910, but realized he was not ready. From there he went on to design and build several of the world's largest airplanes before emigrating to the U.S.A. following the Bolshevik Revolution.

Once on safe ground he set out to build seaplanes and amphibians, several of which were quite successful, though never produced in large numbers. Clearly, the idea of a helicopter had never left his fertile imagination, and in 1940 he demonstrated his VS-300 with its three tail rotors for stability and control, characteristics not common to helicopters that preceded it. He flew it for the newsreel cameras, hovering, flying sideways and backing up, and thus proving it was much more than a preliminary experiment.

Pleased with this progress, Vought-Sikorsky Aircraft then landed an Army contract for a two-seat helicopter to be known

as the XR-4. It flew for the first time in January 1942 on the power of a 165hp Warner Super Scarab radial engine, and was accepted in May, following a 760-mile flight from its Connecticut factory to Wright Field. Seventeen YR-4 prototypes were ordered in January 1943 for use in developing field operations for this novel machine.

Success led to the first combat use of one of the YR-4s to rescue several downed airmen in the China–Burma–India theater of war in April 1944. At about the same time, production R-4s were being operated in support of Aviation Repair boats in the south Pacific, as well as to evacuate badly wounded soldiers. The helicopter was now a useful aerial tool, performing missions not possible for fixed-wing airplanes.

Not only did the USAAF learn how to fly and use helicopters with the R-4, the U.S. Navy received 20 R-4Bs in addition to 7 YR-4Bs as HNS-1from the first production run, and the RAF got 45 to train, among others, pilots and mechanics and mission planners. Most were powered by the uprated 180–200hp Warner R-550 Super Scarab radial engine. In all, some 130 R-4s of all versions were built before they were supplanted by the R-5

Specifications

Length: 33ft 8in
Rotor diameter: 37ft 9in
Height: 12ft 5in
Empty weight: 2,100lb
Maximum speed: 75mph
Service ceiling: 8,000ft

Surviving Examples

R-4B
USAAF 43-46506 – National Museum of the U.S. Air Force
USAAF 43-46534 – Yanks Air Museum, Chino, California
USAAF 43-46565 – Canadian Air & Space Museum
USAAF 43-46592 – U.S. Army Aviation Museum, Ft. Rucker, Alabama

XR-4C
USAAC 41-18874 – U.S. National Air & Space Museum

Hoverfly Mk.I
RAF KL110 – Royal Air Force Museum, Hendon

Sikorsky R-5 /HO2S-1

Almost a year before Sikorsky's pioneering R-4 became the first helicopter to see military action, the prototype of its replacement R-5 had flown. Twenty-six were ordered as YR-5A's for service tests in March 1944 (including two as HO2S-1 for the U.S. Navy), with the first of those being delivered in February 1945. A contract was signed for the production of 100 R-5A with external racks for patient litters, though many were canceled at war's end. By that time, 65 had been built.

Manufacture continued after the war with the highly modified R-5F having a larger rotor and space for a pilot and three passengers. The Navy ordered 46 Sikorsky Model S-51 as its HO3S-1, and Westland Aircraft built several hundred of these improved versions as the Westland-Sikorsky Dragonfly for the RAF and Royal Navy, starting a long relationship between the two companies.

Surviving Examples

YH-5A
USAAF 43-46620 – National Museum of the U.S. Air Force
USAAF 43-47954 – U.S. National Air & Space Museum

Specifications

Length: 41ft 2in
Rotor diameter: 47ft 11in
Height: 12ft 11in
Loaded weight: 4,815lb
Maximum speed: 90mph
Maximum range: 280 miles
Service ceiling: 10,000ft

Sikorsky R-6/ Hoverfly II

The R-6 was a more powerful, better streamlined development of the R-4, with the prototype flying just two months after the first R-5. The XR-6 had a 225hp horizontally-opposed six-cylinder Franklin O-435 engine, with the 5 XR-6A using an up-rated 240hp Franklin O-405. Five prototypes were built, of which three went to the U.S. Navy as XHOS-1.

After the XR-6 and XR-6A had been built by Sikorsky, production was transferred to the Nash–Kelvinator Co., a merger of an automobile and a refrigerator manufacturer. There, 26 YR-6A and

193 R-6A were built, the first being delivered to the U.S. Army in late 1944. A plan to send 150 R-6A to the RAF as the Hoverfly II, were cut to 27 when the shift of manufacturing facilities caused a long delay.

Total production, including prototypes, was 225.

Specifications

Length: 47ft 11in
Rotor diameter: 38ft 0in
Maximum weight: 2,600lb
Maximum speed: 100mph
Service ceiling: 10,000ft

Surviving Examples of the R-6A

USAAF 43-45379 – National Museum of the U.S. Air Force
USAAF 43-45473 – U.S. Army Aviation Museum, Ft. Rucker, Alabama
USAAF 43-45480 – New England Air Museum
USAAF 43-45531 – American Helicopter Museum, W. Chester, Pennsylvania

Kellett R-8

When the XR-1 with its outrigger-mounted twin rotors failed due to its complexity, the U.S. military cast its lot with the single rotor mounted above the fuselage. In an effort to improve the aerodynamics of such helicopters by removing the tail rotor, autogyro builder Kellett suggested using counter-rotating, inter-meshed rotors. Thus was born the egg-shaped XR-8 "egg-beater".

In September 1943, a contract was awarded for the construction of two prototypes, the XR-8 with three-bladed rotors and the XR-8A with two-bladed. The first flight of the XR-8 was in August 1944 and led to the addition of two additional vertical stabilizers to improve the directional stability. Shortly thereafter, an inspection revealed that one blade from either rotor had been in contact during flight; the solution was to have Kellett build two rigid rotors to replace the originals.

While the re-work was underway, the XR-8A flew with a pair of two-bladed rotors, which experienced such severe vibration that no practical solution could be found. Soon it became apparent that the XR-8 would have to undergo a major redesign to fly with the rigid rotors. Not until several months after the end of the war was it accepted for military trials with its original rotor arrangement.

A combination of the prolonged and still unsatisfactory work on the two prototypes, and the much more promising progress with other helicopter designs led to the cancellation of the entire program. Many years later, highly successful helicopters of quite similar fuselage shape and rotor design were produced by Kaman in the U.S.A. and Kamov in the U.S.S.R.

Specifications of the XR-8

Length: 22ft 7in
Rotor Diameter: 36ft 0in
Height: 11ft 0in
Empty weight: 2,320lb
Maximum speed: 100mph
Service ceiling: 6,700ft

Surviving Example

USAAF 43-44714 – U.S. National Air & Space Museum

Great Britain

Cierva C.30-A

The most important, most complicated and often most delicate portion of a rotary-wing aircraft is the rotor hub, which is called on to vary the blade angles in what may seem like a half dozen different ways at the same time. Juan de la Cierva may not have been the first to think about this, but he was the first to attack the problem logically and come up with a solution.

Trying to fly an autogyro like an airplane, with ailerons, rudder and elevators, simply didn't work with the very limited airflow over the control surfaces at the unusually low take-off and landing speeds which were among the aircraft's outstanding characteristics. The only obvious alternative was to move the rotor hub in ways that would affect the autogyro's roll and pitch. This led to new flight controls that had to be moved in a coordinated way by the pilot's already busy hands.

The first autogyro to have a fully controlled rotor system was the C.30, one of which made a 3,000-mile trip around the British Isles and established it as having achieved all its primary goals. Production followed quickly in not only Britain but France (as the Loire-et-Olivier 301), Germany (as the Focke-Wulf C.30), the U.S.A. and elsewhere. The great achievement of the C-30 and its successors was to lead to the first practical helicopters and, paradoxically, to the end of the short story of the autogyro.

In the UK, Avro went into production in 1934, building 78 examples of the C.30A with a 140hp Armstrong Siddeley Genet radial engine providing the forward thrust. A dozen were delivered to the RAF as the Avro 671 Rota Mk.1, while most were sold to individuals and to flying clubs hoping to capitalize on the naively expected rush of pilots wishing to learn to fly them. Others were exported to countries interested in learning more about this new device.

Many of the civilian autogyros were militarized by the RAF when the war started and served in radar calibration duties. When the war ended, those still flyable re-entered civil aviation.

Specifications

Length: 19ft 8in
Rotor diameter: 37ft 0in

Height: 11ft 1in
Empty weight: 1,220lb
Maximum speed: 110mph
Maximum range: 285 miles
Rate of climb: 700ft/min

Surviving Examples

Avro Rota I
RAF K4232 – RAF Museum, Hendon
RAF HM580 – Imperial War Museum, Duxford

C.30
civil I-CIER – Museum of Science and Technology, Milan, Italy

C.30A
RAF AP506 – Helicopter Museum, Weston-super-Mare, England
RAF AP507 – Science Museum, London
RAF H-KX – Fantasy of Flight
civil LN-BAD – Aviodome, Amsterdam
civil VH-USR – Powerhouse Museum, Sydney, Australia

LeO C.302
civil F-BDAD – Musee de l'Air, Paris

Germany

Focke Achgelis FA.330 Sandpiper

As a result of the Earth being round rather than flat, U-boat captains needed some way to extend their vision of the distant sea all the way to the horizon, beyond the 6 miles from the conning tower to 25 miles or more from on high. For the same purpose, surface ships had developed the crow's nest where seamen had the unenviable job of hanging from a small compartment high on a mast. For submarines, which had no such tall masts, one solution was a simple autogyro towed by a long cable to an altitude of 400 feet, where the pilot could see much farther.

The "roto-kite" had no power of its own, relying on the forward motion of its U-boat to force a flow of air over the rotors, providing lift. The "pilot" of the FA.330 communicated with the rest of the crew via a telephone line parallel to the towline. Under normal circumstances, the rotor-kite was raised and lowered with a deck-mounted winch. Upon its return to the deck, the craft was dismantled and stowed in water-tight compartments on the deck.

In case of an emergency requiring a crash-dive, the rotor assembly was jettisoned by the "pilot", automatically opening a parachute for the remainder of the craft, which the "pilot" then cast off, finishing by parachuting into the sea. If the situation permitted, he would then be recovered and transferred into the U-boat. If not, his career ended abruptly.

By the time the FA.330 was ready to join the U-boat fleet, the Allies had assumed control of the air, making the use of the observation technique too risky. It was used briefly in the South Atlantic and the Indian Oceans by at least three U-boats, in areas where air attacks were less likely. There is only a single known example of a ship being sunk thanks to its airborne observation.

After the war, the British used captured FA.330 for experimental purposes, towing them behind ships and even jeeps. The concept, while appealing in its simplicity, produced little and led to nothing.

Specifications

Length: 14ft 7in
Rotor diameter: 24ft
Height: 5ft 6in
Empty weight: 180lb
Normal towing speed: 25mph
Absolute ceiling: 720ft

Surviving Examples

USAAF FE-4618 – U.S. National Air & Space Museum
National Museum of the U.S. Air Force
RAF Museum, Cosford
Luftwaffe 100143 – Imperial War Museum, Duxford
Deutsches Technik Museum, Germany

Nagler Rolz NR-54

This is almost certainly the smallest and slowest powered aircraft ever considered for World War II. "Almost certainly" because it never quite got around to flying.

It was designed and built by Bruno Nagler as a one-man sporting helicopter that could be conveniently folded up and carried in a backpack. One can almost visualize a hunter in the north woods being tracked by a large, angry bear, quickly assembling the 'copter and taking off just in time to escape the long, sharp claws, while giving the bear another tall tale to tell its cubs that evening. But from a purely practical standpoint, very simple rotorcraft often are revealed in practice to be difficult to fly by other than very experienced pilots, though they are promoted as just the opposite.

When the German Air Ministry heard about the idea, it proposed a military version having an 8hp engine mounted roughly mid-way

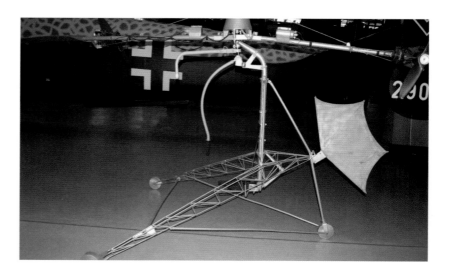

between the hub and the tip of either blade and eliminating torque problems faced by other helicopters. Due to the great centrifugal force created by the blades whirling at 6,000 rpm, it proved impossible to regulate the flow of fuel to the engine's carburetor. No one ever knew what other problems might be revealed by test flights, as none of the four prototypes got that far.

Specifications

Length: 7ft 11in
Rotor diameter: 26ft 3in
Height: 7ft 2in
Empty weight: 81lb
Cruising speed: estimated 50mph
Maximum range: estimated 50–60 miles
Rate of climb: estimated 460ft/min

Surviving Example

c/n V2 – U.S. National Air & Space Museum, Dulles Airport, Virginia

Flettner Fl.282 Hummingbird

It could have been the most important helicopter of World War II, had not an Allied bombing raid flattened the BMW factory which had just started large-scale production.

Flettner had achieved the first success with an intermeshing rotor arrangement in 1939, building and flying six test versions of its German Navy-backed Fl.265, powered by the reliable 150hp Siemens-Halske radial engine. Fifteen prototypes were ordered, with flight tests in 1941 including take-offs and landings from a helipad on a cruiser and were hoped to lead to a larger order for submarine spotting duties. A submarine-based version never got beyond the planning stage.

The first two had closed cockpits, while the rest had open cockpits, possibly for improved visibility for the sole occupant. Other proposed uses included inter-ship communication, and reconnaissance. The two-seat Fl.282B proved useful to the Army for artillery spotting. The helicopter had a bright future. Had the factory remained serviceable after the first 24 production machines had been completed, the type might have become well known.

Of those built, most served in a single unit as artillery spotters, though with a cruising speed of just 50mph, it was an easy target for small arms fire, and if caught by surprise, for Soviet air Force fighters, although it could outmaneuver these if given a chance.

Specifications

Length: 21ft 6in
Rotor diameter: 39ft 3in
Height: 7ft 3in
Empty weight: 1,675lb
Maximum speed: 93mph
Maximum range: 100 miles
Service ceiling: 10,800ft
Rate of climb: 1,500ft/min

Surviving Examples

Fl-282-V10
Luftwaffe 28368 – Midland Air Museum

Chapter 7

Amphibian Utility

This is a sub-category of "Utility", for amphibious aircraft used for photography, target-towing, scouting and for air-sea rescue operations. In general, while they proved to be faster than small boats, they were not as seaworthy.

United States of America

Grumman J2F/OA-12 Duck

The Duck traces its lineage back to the U.S. Navy's OL, designed by aviation pioneer Grover Loening and easily recognized by its resemblance to a flying boat, thanks to the fuselage sides having been extended downward to the main float for better streamlining. As many as 180 were built from 1925 to 1929: 125 as OLs for the Navy and 55 as OA-1s and -2s for the Army. Loening then merged with the Keystone Aircraft Corp.

The OLs and OAs were replaced in service by the visually similar Grumman JF Duck, of which 48 were built for the U.S. Navy, Marine Corps and Coast Guard. The OL first flew in April 1933 and was built in 1936. All were powered by Pratt & Whitney's 800hp R-1830 Twin Wasp radial engines.

The basic aircraft had space for a pilot, radio operator and observer under the long canopy, and for two passengers or one stretcher patient lower in the fuselage.

In April 1936, the first prototype of the improved J2F-1 made its initial flight, powered by a 750hp Wright R-1820 Cyclone 9. Deliveries of 29 of them began almost immediately and were soon followed by 21 for the U.S. Marine Corps with machine guns in the nose and rear of the cockpit, as well as racks for several small bombs under the wings.

Specifications

Length: 34ft 0in
Wingspan: 39ft 0in
Height: 13ft 11in
Wing area: 409 sq ft
Empty weight: 5,480lb
Maximum speed: 190mph
Maximum range: 780 miles
Service ceiling: 20,000ft

Surviving Examples

USNM,
Planes of Fame,
Civil N1196N– Experimental Aircraft Association Museum
Fantasy of Flight
USAAF 43-2680 – J2F-6 (as OA-10) – National Museum of the U.S.
  Air Force

The J2F-2A, of which nine were built, had some changes for use in the U.S. Virgin Islands, and in 1939, 20 more were built as the J2F-3 with an uprated engine and were fitted out as executive transports. Thirty-two of the J2F-4 variant were equipped for towing targets, and the major Grumman-built version – the J2F-5 – used a 1,050hp Wright R-1820. One of these went to the USAAF in 1942.

With the start of the war, Grumman suddenly found itself under great pressure to produce as many F4F Wildcat fighters and TBF Avenger torpedo bombers as possible, which left no production capacity for Duck amphibians. Thus, the most plentiful production version, the J2F-6, was turned over to Columbia Aircraft, which built 330 with the more powerful engine, bomb racks and towing gear. Later, eight of these, which had been declared surplus by the Navy, reappeared as USAAF OA-12s.

Grumman JRF-/OA-13 Goose

Grumman's transition from its classic U.S. Navy biplanes to modern streamlined monoplanes came in the form of its Goose amphibian, first ordered by a group of wealthy New York sportsmen who needed a way to travel to inconvenient hunting and fishing spots in greater comfort than was supplied by current aircraft. The result was Grumman's first production monoplane, first twin-engined aircraft, and the start of a long line of successful water-borne craft.

The first Goose flew in May 1937, followed immediately by a dozen Model G-21s using a pair of 450hp Pratt & Whitney R-985

Wasp Jr radial engines. They were early executive transports, with two or three comfortable seats, a bar and a small toilet. In 1938, the USAAF ordered 26 as the OA-9 with more seats and fewer amenities. Later, three civil G-21As were impressed as OA-13A, and two JRF-5s were transferred to the USAAF as OA-13B.

The U.S. Navy entered the picture in 1938 by ordering a single XJ3F-1 prototype eight-seat utility amphibian, which led to the production JRF-1, of which five more were built. Small groups of variously modified Gooses (or Geese?) were bought by the Navy and U.S. Coast Guard, culminating in an order for 184 examples of the JRF-5 which incorporated the JRF-1A's target-towing and camera equipment, the JRF-3's de-icer equipment, and the JRF-4's bomb racks.

All through the war, several hundred JRFs were operated by the Navy and Coast Guard, and OA-10s by the Army on a wide variety of missions, including transport, reconnaissance, training, air-sea rescue, and general utility. The Fleet Air Arm used three JRF-5s (as the Goose Mk.I), and 44 JRF-6B's (as Goose Mk.IA), while two JRF-5s (as Mk. II) were flown as staff transports for the British Air Commission in the U.S.A. and Canada.

After the war, the Goose proved popular with civil operators needing a machine with its versatility and reliability. Later, many were modified with everything from two or four six-cylinder Lycoming piston engines to a pair of Pratt & Whitney of Canada PT6A turboprops Some continue to serve today.

Specifications

Length: 38ft 6in
Wingspan: 49ft 0in
Height: 16ft 2in

Wing area: 375 sq ft
Empty weight: 5,425lb
Maximum speed: 230mph
Maximum range: 640 miles
Service ceiling: 21,300ft
Rate of climb: 1,100ft/min

Surviving Examples

U.S. Coast Guard V190 – U.S. National Museum of Naval Aviation
Civil NC-702A – U.S. National Air & Space Museum

Grumman J4F/OA-14 Widgeon

After the success of the Goose, Grumman developed a smaller, generally similar version for the civilian market, the G-44 Widgeon, with two 200hp Ranger L-440 inverted inline, six-cylinder engines. The first G-44 was designed in 1939 and flew for the first time in 1940.

In July 1941 the first of 25 built for the U.S. Coast Guard as the J4F-1 was delivered as a three-seat modification of the civil G-44. In 1942, the first of 131 J4F-2, with five seats, entered service with the U.S. Navy, which equipped them with shackles to carry a 375-lb depth charge for anti-submarine operations. The USAAF acquired 15 civil Widgeons by impressments, called the OA-14, which was joined by one OA-14A for the Army Corps of Engineers.

Fifteen of the Navy's J4F-2s were sent to the Royal Navy, which first called them Gosling before reverting to the type's original name. Forty-one more G-44s were built under license in France after the war as the SCAN 30.

Many Widgeons were sold as war surplus and used for a wide variety of purposes, many of which required extensive modifications, including a re-shaped hull for improved water handling, up to six additional seats, and a variety of more powerful engines. Seventy "Super Widgeons" were powered by two 270hp Lycoming GO-480, and offered much more modern avionics and even retractable wingtip floats. Many of these remain in commercial use.

Specifications

Length: 31ft 1in
Wingspan: 40ft 0in
Height: 11ft 5in
Wing area: 245 sq ft
Empty weight: 3,190lb
Maximum speed: 160mph
Maximum range: 920 miles
Service ceiling: 14,600ft
Rate of climb: 1,000ft/min

Surviving Examples

J4F-1
BuAer unk. – U.S. Museum of Naval Aviation

J4F-2
BuAer 32976 – Pima Air and Space Museum

Northrop N3PB Nomad

When, in 1938, Nazi Germany began occupying its less warlike neighbors, the Norwegians decided it was time to modernize and enlarge their Army and Navy air services. Two dozen float-equipped monoplanes based on the Northrop A-17 were purchased, but could not be delivered as Norway had been added to the Third Reich following the invasion in April 1940.

The N-3PB started out as a Douglas 8A-5N, but when it became apparent that it could not be equipped with the floats Norway considered vital, the newly re-organized Northrop Aircraft Co.

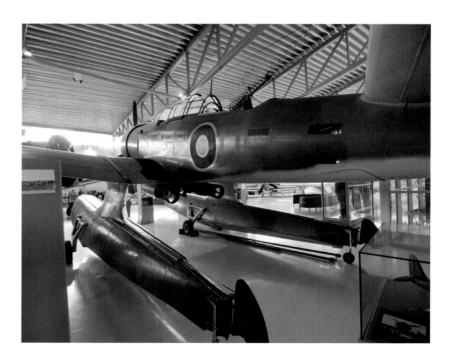

entered the picture, offering to design and build a floatplane based on the 8A-5N. Changes to make it suitable for coastal reconnaissance included modifying the twin floats so that a torpedo or bombs could be carried below the fuselage, and changing the armament to four Norwegian-built .50 cal. machine guns in the wings and two .30 cal. machine guns to be operated by the rear-seat gunner.

The first test fight of the prototype was in December 1940 with a more powerful engine than originally planned: a 1,200hp nine-cylinder Wright R-1820 radial. All 24 N-3PBs were delivered to the exile Royal Norwegian Navy Air Service within three months. Six went to one of the Canadian "Little Norway" training bases, while the others were shipped to a Norwegian RAF squadron in Iceland.

Anti-submarine patrols and convoy escort were flown from June 1941 until February 1943, when British Short Sunderland flying boats replaced them as well as several PBY Catalinas. The big boats had greater range and load-carrying capacity. Three N-3PBs were sent to Scotland, while the others were scrapped.

Those based in western Canada were used as advanced trainers for Norwegian pilots until it was determined that those pilots were to join regular RAF squadrons and so needed training in more appropriate airplanes. After the war ended, the two surviving Northrop float planes were flown to Norway and scrapped. The only survivor was recovered from an Icelandic river and restored to like-new condition by Northrop Aircraft volunteers, including some who had worked on the type in 1941.

Specifications

Length: 36ft 0in
Wingspan: 48ft 11in
Height: 12ft 0in

Wing area: 377 sq ft
Empty weight: 6,190lb
Maximum speed: 257mph
Maximum range: 1,000 miles
Service ceiling: 24,000ft
Rate of climb: 1,000ft/min

Surviving Example

Norwegian Armed Forces Aircraft Collection, Gerdermoen

Great Britain

Supermarine Walrus

When it entered squadron service in 1935 it was the first British military aircraft to have fully-retractable landing gear, a fully-enclosed cockpit and an all-metal fuselage. It eventually became one of the last biplanes to be produced and used by any country's military. It can trace its ancestry back to the Supermarine Seal, a similar looking naval aircraft that first flew prior to 1921. Its rugged structure and surprising agility enabled the Walrus to perform useful service long after sleek monoplanes had become all the rage.

The Walrus' immediate predecessor was the Seagull, the first of which was a modified Seal II, and flew in 1921. More than 30 Seagulls were built and most served as catapult-launched scouts for the Fleet Air Arm, while others were used by the Royal Australian Air Force. The Seagull V then became the Walrus, and while it was the same over-all size, it was much faster and had a greater rate of climb, thanks to superior streamlining and a 680hp Bristol Pegasus

The main function of the Walrus was supposed to have been spotting for the naval artillery, but turned out to be searching for German U-boats and surface ships. This was soon made easier by the installation of Air-to-Surface Vessel radar. In a few instances they were even used to attack land targets with bombs and machine guns. Others were used to rescue aircrew downed at sea.

A replacement for the Walrus was being developed as early as 1938, though it was not ready until 1942. The Supermarine Sea Otter was slightly larger, much heavier and more powerful, giving it a substantially higher speed. But while several hundred were delivered to the FAA and RAF, the Walrus was not retired and managed to serve alongside the newer design right to the end of the war.

Specifications

Length: 33ft 7in
Wingspan: 45ft 10ft
Height: 15ft 3in
Wing area: 610 sq ft
Empty weight: 4,900lb
Maximum speed: 135mph
Maximum range: 600 miles
Service ceiling: 18,500ft
Rate of climb: 1,050ft/min

Surviving Example

FAA L2301 – Fleet Air Arm Museum
RAAF HD874 – Royal Australian Air Force Museum

radial in place of the 480hp Napier Lion V-12 – and to the design genius of R.J. Mitchell.

Defensive armament consisted of a single .30 cal. machine gun in the nose and one in the rear. For offensive purposes, it could carry up to 760lb of depth charges and/or bombs slung from fittings under the wings.

The first production order came in 1935 for 24 Seagull V for the Royal Australian Air Force, to be catapulted off cruisers and then hoisted back onboard by crane. The RSAF then began placing orders for the Walrus Mk.I, the first of which flew in 1936.

Due to the rapidly increasing demand for Vickers-Supermarine's Spitfire, manufacturing of the Walrus Mk.I and the wooden-hulled Mk.II were shifted to Saunders Roe, another firm with long experience building watercraft.

Germany

Dornier Do.24

The Do.24 is unquestionably a German aircraft, though arriving at that conclusion can be confusing. It started out as a Dutch aircraft built in Germany, then became an American-powered German aircraft built in the Netherlands, then a German aircraft built in France, and finally a French aircraft built in France.

The immediate forerunner of the Do.24 was Dornier's Do.17 Wal, a twin-engined flying boat that pioneered transatlantic airmail service. More than 250 of the highly reliable Wals were built in Italy, Spain, Japan, The Netherlands and finally Germany, and some served until 1950.

By the mid-1930s the need for a similar flying boat that could be used for military purposes – air-sea rescue and maritime patrol – had led to the more streamlined, more powerful Do.24. The first prototype, powered by a trio of Wright Cyclone engines, flew in July 1937, and soon led to an order from the Dutch Government for flying boats to be used in the Dutch East Indies.

Six Do.24s had been built in Germany and 25 in the Netherlands when Germany conquered and occupied its neighbor. Production continued, though with German Bramo engines, in the original factory, but under German control and for the German military. Once the war had begun, the main use for the big boat was to rescue downed Luftwaffe crews.

Those delivered to the Dutch East Indies were first used against the Japanese and then operated by the Royal Australian Air Force in the transport role. It was a rare example of one type of aircraft being used in quantity by both the Axis and the Allies, with a few being operated by neutrals, Sweden and Spain.

Of more than 275 built during and just after the war, a few continued to be operated as civil aircraft into the late 1960s. In 2004, a modernized and rebuilt Do.24 ATT was flown around the world on behalf of a United Nations agency concerned with children.

Specifications

Length: 72ft 2in
Wingspan: 88ft 6in
Height: 19ft 3ft
Wing area: 1,162 sq ft
Empty weight: 29,700lb
Maximum speed: 212mph
Maximum range: 3,600 miles

Service ceiling: 19,350ft
Maximum bomb load: 1,300lb

Surviving Examples

Do.24T-3
EC-DAF – Dutch Air Force Museum, Soesterburg (on loan from
   RAF Museum)
Luftwaffe KS+FA – Deutsches Museum, Obserschleissheim,
   Germany
N99240 – Museo del Aire, Cuatro Vientos, Spain

Chapter 8

Research and Record Setting

Research aircraft are meant for studying basic new ideas, and are not simply stepping stones to eventual series production. Experimental aircraft are, with a few exceptions, meant to be the initial testing vehicles for future production airplanes having some similar characteristics. All U.S. military and naval aircraft whose designations begin with "X" are in the experimental category. Most such aircraft carry manufacturer's designations, which can cause considerable confusion.

but he went on to demonstrate the flying capabilities of the novel idea with aeromodels.

With the approach of war, Government officials responsible for doling out research and development funds became increasingly willing to back what otherwise would have been considered some pretty outlandish ideas. If even one of them panned out, major advances just might result. Zimmerman was by then working for Chance Vought, and so money was made available in 1941 for what

United States of America

Chance Vought V-173 "Flying Pancake"
While fuselages are of unquestionable value in carrying engines, crews, payloads and tails, there has always been the suspicion that an airplane without a fuselage would be superior. If all the necessary items could be crowded into a wing, the overall wind resistance should be much lower. Hence the periodic attempts to create flying wings.

One of the less conventional efforts was that of former NACA engineer Charley Zimmerman, who saw a future in an airplane having an oval shape, with an aspect ratio of less than 1:1. As early as 1933 he won a NACA design competition with just such a craft having an oval shape and almost no wingspan. It was never built,

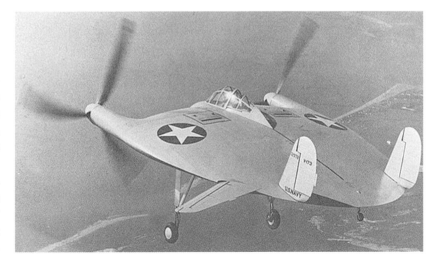

became the V-173, nick-named the "Flying Pancake" for obvious reasons.

The strange looking machine made its first test flight in November 1942 from Chance Vought's factory north of New York City. Once a not-unexpected series of problems was ironed out, the V-173 proceeded not unlike more conventional research airplanes, with a cautious expansion of the flight envelope. The goal had become a highly modified version as a U.S. Navy carrier-based fighter with a most unusual planned speed range of 0-to-500mph: the XF5U-1.

Powered by a pair of 80hp, four-cylinder engines that previously had been used in two-seat personal airplanes, the V-173 was able to reach 138mph despite its size and very large and draggy landing gear. Charles Zimmerman's dream had come true: his omega-shaped airplane worked well enough to justify two prototypes of the fighter, to be powered by a pair of 1,350hp Pratt & Whitney engines driving articulated propellers that were expected to function much like a helicopter's rotors at low speed. For armament, it was to carry up to six 20mm cannon mounted in the leading edges of the "wings".

The V-173 was retired in June 1947 after many flights (including several by Charles Lindbergh and at least one by an admiral). By then, however, the F5U-1 project had gone the way of many others, succumbing to the far greater appeal of more conventional airframes using the exciting new turbojet engines. It was broken up after a couple of high-speed taxi tests during which it is said to have climbed to an altitude of several feet.

Specifications

Length: 26ft 8in
Wingspan: 23ft 4in

Height: 12ft 11in
Wing area: 427 sq ft
Maximum weight: 2,260lb
Maximum speed: 138mph
Rate of climb: 5,000ft in 7:00

Sole Surviving Example

BuAer 02978 – U.S. National Air & Space Museum

Northrop N-1M

John K. Northrop had dreamed of building a pure flying wing without any semblance of a tail and paving the way for much more efficient airplanes by doing away with not only tails but fuselages. It was a dream that would direct his life to the end, and which would not see fruition until after his death at 85.

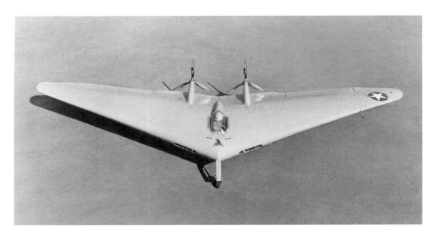

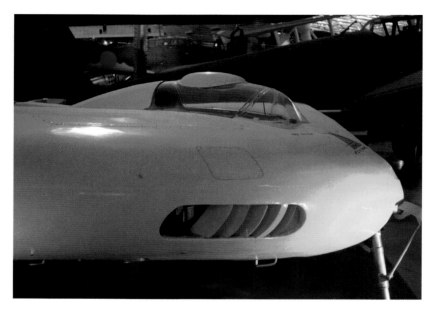

After great success with Douglas and Lockheed, where he designed the World Cruiser and Vega, he formed his own company and refined his designs that featured cantilever wings and all-metal stressed-skin construction. But flying wings were always in the background, with the first attempt flying in 1929. While it had a simple tail supported by thin booms, and the pilot and engine in the thick wing, it was the first step.

Any true flying wing comes with, among many other issues, complex control and stability problems which must be solved if the goal is to be reached. It wasn't until 1939 that Northrop thought he had the problems solved, or at least reduced to manageable proportions. His N-1M had nothing but a wing, though the tips slanted down so that the ailerons could serve additionally as rudders.

The N-1M flew in July 1940 at what would become Muroc Army Air Base, far out in the Mojave Desert of southern California, as U.S. Army Air Corps engineers saw it as the prototype of some future long-range heavy bomber . It was easily the most futuristic airplane the U.S. military had ever considered, and, surprisingly, it flew very well in the hands of several test pilots.

In some 200 fights, it was used to investigate a wide variety of situations uncommon to conventional airplanes. When it had been determined that the down-turned wing tips were less than ideal, they were replaced by split ailerons, which could also be used as a powerful brake to retard the wing in the direction of the desired turn.

The original pair of 65hp four-cylinder Lycoming engines provided insufficient thrust and were soon replaced by 120hp, six-cylinder Franklin engines, which turned three-bladed, variable-pitch propellers. Both engines were then popular among manufacturers of small personal airplanes.

The sole N-1M was one of the most successful of radical designs, and was retired without ever having been seriously damaged in an accident. It was replaced by the larger N-9M, which eventually led to the B-2 stealth bomber.

Specifications

Length: 7ft 11in
Wingspan: 38ft 8in
Height: 4ft 11in
Wing area: 300 sq ft
Loaded weight: 3,900lb

Maximum speed: 200mph
Maximum range: 300 miles
Service ceiling: 4,000ft

Surviving Example

Civil NX-28311 – U.S. National Air & Space Museum

Northrop N-9M

The clear success of Northrop's first true flying wing, the N-1M, was followed by the U.S. Army Air Corps issuing a preliminary order for what would become the huge XB-35 bomber, which would compete with the Convair B-36. Part of the plan was to build a series of ⅓-span scale, piloted versions of the B-35 with which to completely solve the remaining control and stability problems and to acclimatize service pilots to the novel characteristics of an all-wing airplane.

The first N-9M, powered by two 275hp six-cylinder, inline Menasco C6S-4 Buccaneer engines that had previously been used mainly in Thompson Trophy Racers, flew in late December 1942. Much of the structure was of wood to save weight, though the cockpit section was built up from steel tubes. Flight testing went well, with 45 flights being made in the next few months, though most of them experienced problems with the engines. Thus the fourth example – N-9M-B – used more reliable 300hp six-cylinder, horizontally-opposed engines.

In May 1943, the first of the N-9Ms crashed, killing its pilot, who apparently had gotten into a spin from which he had been unable to recover. Following the crash investigation, the control-reversal that was suspected of being the cause, was corrected. Testing continued and led to advances in major areas of a flying wing's special characteristics, including flight on auto-pilot.

With the knowledge thus gained, Northrop proceeded with a variety of flying wing projects. The XP-56 tail-less fighter, at least on paper, should have been one of the fastest piston-engined airplanes ever. But one was lost in a crash, and the other had so many problems that it was retired without ever having completed a really successful flight. The MX-324 was about as streamlined a manned aircraft as could be imagined and was propelled by a small rocket motor. It made its first flight in July 1944, after being towed aloft by a Lockheed P-38. It flew well and fast, but never had a satisfactory motor.

Next came the XP-79 Ram Wing, which was intended to slice off an enemy airplane's wing in combat. Like the MX-324, it had its pilot lying prone. It flew in September 1945, with pilot Harry Crosby putting on an impressive demonstration of control and maneuverability until it suddenly dove into the ground.

The purpose of the N-9M program was to pave the way for the giant XB-35 bomber, which it did well. A half dozen were built and there is movie footage of several flying in formation. Unfortunately, political pressure is said to have played a large role in the B-36 being instead selected for large-scale production. Not even the conversion to jets for the XB-49 could help, as the conversion of B-35s and the construction of new B-49s was canceled. It wasn't until the birth of the B-2 stealth bomber was John Northrop able to rest in peace, knowing he had been right, all along.

Specifications

Length: 17ft 9in
Wingspan: 60ft 0in

Height: 6ft 7in
Wing area: 490 sq ft
Empty weight: 5,893lb
Maximum speed: 258mph
Maximum range: 500 miles
Service ceiling: 21,500ft

Surviving Example

Civil N9MB – Planes of Fame

Great Britain

Gloster E.28/39

The invention of radar may have had a greater impact on the outcome of World War II than any other new idea. But the turbojet engine had the greatest long-term impact on both wartime and peacetime aviation. In September 1939 the Luftwaffe flew the world's first turbojet airplane – the Heinkel He-178 – and in the same month, Britain's Air Ministry ordered its first such machine.

The primary purpose of the Gloster was to test Britain's first jet engine, the Frank Whittle-designed Power Jets W.1, rated at 860lb of thrust. An otherwise perfectly conventional airplane, it made its first flight in May 1941 and quickly proved the usefulness of the strange-sounding engine. New and improved models of the same basic engine were installed during the test program and soon made it necessary to add auxiliary vertical fins to the horizontal stabilizer.

A second prototype joined the test program in March 1943, and, with a 1,500-thrust-pound version of the latest W.2 engine, reached 466mph at high altitude. It was destroyed the following July due to a mechanical problem, though the pilot parachuted to safety. The first E.28/39's flight test program extended into 1944, by which time more capable, mature designs had become reality and the pioneering British jet could be put out to pasture.

In its place came Gloster's second propless airplane, the Meteor, a twin-jet craft with guns and armor and all those things that make up a true military airplane. One of them was the victor in the first jet-to-jet aerial combat, thus introducing the world to a new way of dealing with those having sorely differing views of life.

Specifications

Length: 25ft 4in
Wingspan: 29ft 0in

Height: 8ft 10in
Wing area: 146 sq ft
Empty weight: 2,885lb
Maximum speed: 338mph
Maximum range: 410 miles
Service ceiling: 32,000ft
Rate of climb: 1,060ft/min

Surviving Example

RAF W4041 – Science Museum, South Kensington, London

Germany

Messerschmitt Me-209V

Like other fascinating designs in Great Britain, France, Italy, Germany, Japan and the U.S.A. in the late 1930s that were meant to break the World Absolute Speed Record, the Me-209V was designed to use the largest possible engine, crammed into the smallest, lightest, cleanest airframe that could contain the engine, the pilot, the fuel tanks and a few other obviously vital parts.

That record – 440.667mph, with the Macchi-Castoldi M.C.72 racing *seaplane* – had stood since 1934. It had tempted and challenged many of the world's top designers, who had produced a series of fanciful and realistic designs, some of which were built, many under the guise of military prototypes, which enabled them to proceed despite the gathering war clouds.

In Germany, the need was for more than the pride in technical achievement to be realized with a new official speed mark, but also the propaganda value if the record-breaking airplane could be made to appear to be no more than a modification of a production fighter. It was to this end that the German aircraft industry applied itself.

Just such a modified production airplane was used by Germany to set a new record for land-based airplanes: 379.63mph, in 1937 with a Me-109V prototype of what would soon be the Luftwaffe's primary fighter. But more was needed, and so both Heinkel and Messerschmitt put their engineers to work on an airplane built purely for speed, rather than combat.

On March 30, 1939, the Heinkel He-100V-8 fighter prototype appeared, built with such extensive modifications that the pilot said "flying it was like balancing an egg on the tip of your finger!" Knowing that its fierce rival, Messerschmitt, was preparing to attack

The average speed was faster than the latest record, at 469.22mph, though it was less than the FAI's minimum of 1 per cent. Regardless, the record was accepted by the FAI, with the result that the official and permanent records of the attempt identify the airplane as a Me-109R. Its use as a combat airplane, or even as an early step in that direction, is hard to imagine, as it handled very poorly on the ground and in the air, and its cooling system consisted of skin-surface radiators which would have been highly susceptible to battle damage.

The German Propaganda Ministry, under Josef Goebbels, trumpeted the achievement as proof of the all-conquering superiority of Luftwaffe fighters, no doubt knowing that what would soon be called World War II was to begin in a few months, and that fear would be one of Germany's main weapons.

The Me-209V-1 was on display in the Berlin Air Museum, until it was burned out by an RAF bombing raid in 1943. The surviving parts gradually made their way to the museum in Poland, where they have been preserved in hopes of full restoration in the future.

Specifications

Length: 23ft 9in
Wingspan: 25ft 7in
Wing area: 114 sq ft
Take-off weight: 4,770lb
Maximum speed: 469mph

Surviving Example

German civil D-INJR – Polish National Air Museum, Krakow

the Absolute Record, Heinkel got the edge by flying first. Four runs by Hans Dieterle produced an average speed of 463.95mph, well over the 1 per cent minimum increase required by the International Aeronautics Federation (FAI).

Three weeks later, the very difficult to fly Messerschmitt Me-209V-1 was ready for its attempt, and there the picture becomes murky. No foreign (meaning FAI) observers were permitted, though required by agreed-upon rules. And while another rule stated that four consecutive, opposite-direction runs were to be made without landing, there is evidence that Messerschmitt pilot Fritz Wendel landed after each 3km dash, as his highly modified Daimler-Benz DB.601 was prone to severe over-heating.

Lippisch DM-1

The first project for which Alexander Lippisch is known is Messershmitt's Me.163 rocket-powered, swept-wing, tail-less interceptor, capable of more than 600mph in 1944. This success allowed him to think in terms of supersonic and even hypersonic (Mach 5+) airplanes. His first such design was the DM-1, a delta-winged glider for the purpose of exploring the problems of such a shape at very high and very low speeds. He envisioned that an airplane with this airframe layout and with never-specified power, might reach Mach 6, or almost 4,000mph. The DM-4 was to have a top speed of 10,000mph, or Mach 15! Needless to say, neither the DM-4 nor any successor was ever built, let alone flown.

The DM-1's construction was interrupted by an Allied bombing raid, and the unfinished prototype was found by the British and American Armies sweeping across Germany in the Spring of 1945. U.S, intelligence experts were particularly interested in the project and arranged to have it completed and the shipped to the NACA laboratories at Langley, Virginia for tests in the full-scale wind tunnel.

Knowledge thus acquired by NACA was passed along to airplane manufacturers and is said to have played a role in the design and development of a series of Convair delta-winged fighters from the XF-92 through to the F-106. Other delta-shaped fighters and bombers which may have been inspired by the work of Lippisch range from the French Mirages to the Convair B-58 Hustler to the ultimate, the Anglo-French Concorde Mach 2 supersonic transport.

The DM-1's construction is perfectly conventional, consisting of a steel tubing structure covered with plywood.

Specifications

Length: 21ft 7in
Wingspan: 19ft 5in
Height: 10ft 5in
Wing area: 204 sq ft
Empty weight: 655lb
Maximum speed:
Glide ratio: 7:1

Surviving Example

National Air & Space Museum

Horten III

Brothers Walter and Reimar were designers and builders of high-performance sailplanes that featured slightly-swept-back wings, and neither fuselages nor tails. They began work on such craft around 1930 and continued through World War II. There is some reason to believe that they were able to finance some of their later designs by convincing the German Air Ministry that these sailplanes had military potential.

The Horten I was built in 1931–32 and had a brief life before being burned by the brothers; it had an unswept wing. The Horten II was built in 1933–34 as a larger and improved Type I, that was first flown as a glider and then with an 80hp Hirth inline engine turning a pusher propeller; it was successful in soaring competitions.

In 1937 or 1938, the brothers built their Type III, which was used to test a wide variety of wing flaps and control surfaces in the sub-types –B and –C. Based on the Types I and II, it had a wing with higher aspect ratio (thinness, as seen from the top) and thus performed better as a sporting sailplane. The avowed goal of the craft was the 1938 Rhön gliding competition, in which both Type IIIa crashed, one of them fatally.

The Type IIId was a IIIb with a new center section for the pilot and a 32hp Volkswagen engine with a folding propeller. The Type IIIe was equipped with variable-sweep and variable-dihedral wings. Three Type IIIfs were built with provisions for a prone pilot. The IIIh had a second cockpit for test equipment, and its center section, including the cockpit, is the sole survivor.

The Luftwaffe funded four III's, none of which performed well in competition, in one case due to its pilot's hangover. Other government Type IIIs were tested as ammunition carriers, for which it would seem to have been poorly qualified. No doubt sensing the eventual success of some development of these sporting sailplanes, the Luftwaffe acquired several Type IIIg two-seaters which were built as trainers, while yet others were employed to test control systems. Despite the lack of success, the Horten brothers continued their efforts to create more efficient sailplanes and then, as war became a reality, military designs.

Specifications of the IIIa

Length: 16ft 5in
Wingspan: 66ft 11in
Height: 5ft 3in
Wing area: 390 sq ft
Empty weight: 485lb
Maximum speed: 130mph
Glide ratio: 28:1

Surviving Example

Luftwaffe D-10-125 – U.S. National Air & Space Museum

Horten IV

The Type IV was the logical next step beyond the Type III, and had a much greater aspect ratio wing for improved soaring performance. It was designed specifically to be tested against more conventional sailplanes, and so one was built and flown in 1941, and another three in 1943. Several were flown in unofficial German competitions, with good results.

To reduce aerodynamic drag even further than by the basic flying-wing shape, the pilot was placed in the prone position. The cockpit was designed to fit the original test pilot, and turned out to be too small for the next pilot, and had to be enlarged considerably.

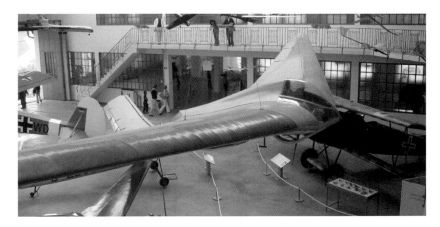

Wing area: 203 sq ft
Empty weight: 540lb
Maximum speed: 125mph
Glide ratio: 32:1

Surviving Examples

c/n 25 – Planes of Fame
c/n 26 – Deutsches Museum, Oberschleissheim, Germany

Horten VI

This was the final true sailplane designed by the Horten brothers, and featured what may well be the highest aspect ratio – 32:1 – in the history of the sport. Its purpose was to create the highest performance sailplane at any cost, and probably succeeded, as it out-performed the conventional D.30, until then considered the ultimate.

The first of two Type VI was flight tested in late 1944, when it was becoming obvious that the end of Nazi Germany was in sight, and it was just as obvious that the time and effort being used in such projects as this could be better spent on desperate attempts to prevent the Allies from achieving total domination of German skies.

In addition to the surviving Horten gliders mentioned here, the U.S. National Air & Space Museum is having four more restored by the Deutsches Technik Museum in Berlin: a Ho.II, Ho.IIIf, and a Ho.IIIh.

The Horten brothers post-Type VI efforts were highly varied but produced nothing of military consequence, despite their intriguing potential:

Flying from this position does not appear to have posed any major problems, though the stick design is highly unconventional. Upon take-off, the wheels are attached to a dolly, which is then dropped. For landing, the retractable front skid is lowered and works along with the fixed rear skid.

A Type IVb was built with a laminar-flow airfoil copied from a captured P-51 Mustang, but fell short of directional stability. It could not be tested sufficiently due to the war ending. A Type IIIc reverted to the original airfoil shape.

After the war, two or three of the Type IV were taken to Great Britain and the U.S.A. where they were flown in civilian soaring contests, where they acquitted themselves well.

Specifications

Length: 12ft 6in
Wingspan: 66ft 7in

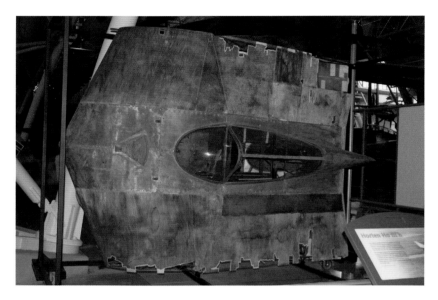

Ho.VII – An enlarged Type V with a more prominent fuselage and two 240hp Argus piston engines. Two were built and flown as prototype communications airplanes shortly before the Allies captured the factory.

Ho.VIII – A 160-foot span, 60-passenger airliner with six 600hp BMW engines driving pusher propellers. It was optimistically scheduled for its first flight in November 1945, which turned out to be six months after the war's end.

Ho.IX – A twin-jet fighter-bomber described in Volume I of this series.

Ho.X – Either a Type III with moveable wingtip control surfaces, or a glider with sharply swept-back wings.

Ho.XI – A single seat aerobatic glider with 25-foot wings.

Ho.XII – Probably similar to a Type III, but with side-by-side seating and a 50hp engine.

Ho. XIII – The largest of the Horten military designs, it was a 100-foot span flying wing bomber to be powered by four BMW or Junkers turbojet engines and using one of the first multiple-wheel landing gears.

Ho. XVIII – The 130-foot wingspan "Amerika bomber", whose six engines were supposed to get it to New York or Washington with a nuclear bomb, but both the airplane and the bomb were far from realization when the war ended in May 1945.

Specifications

Length: 8ft 3in
Wingspan: 79ft 5in
Height: 3ft 4in
Empty weight: 725lb
Maximum speed: 125mph

Surviving Example

USAAF TE-5040 – U.S. National Air & Space Museum

Italy

Caproni-Campini CC.2 or N.1

It could almost pass for a fairly modern turbojet-powered airplane, as long as no one removed any cowling panels and bared the radial piston engine mounted a few feet aft of the nose air intake. Briefly claimed by the Italian Air Force as the first jet to fly, it had actually followed the German He-178, by a full year. While the piston engine did not prevent it from producing all its thrust by jet reaction, it was definitely not a turbojet in any sense of the term. In order for that to have been the case, it needed its own compressor, not one run by an engine intended to turn a propeller.

Italian interest in developing a jet engine dates back to 1931, when Secondo Campini designed an airplane powered by a jet-thrust engine whose power came from a 670hp Isotta Fraschini L.121 radial piston engine, and was a lot like a big afterburner. His work led to a government contract to build to airplanes to be powered by what was then called a thermo-jet engine.

Progress was slow, due to technical problems and increasing costs, but the first CC.2 (also called the N.1) finally made its first 10-minute flight in August 1940. The second airplane flew in April 1941, and in November of that year made a flight from Milan to Rome at all of 135mph.

An Italian airplane had flown on the thrust created by a blast of hot air out its large tailpipe, making Italy the second country to do so. But it had not used a true turbojet engine, and while testing continued well into 1942, nothing came of it. Italy did not produce a jet until well after the end of World War II, and then it bore no resemblance to the CC.2 in appearance or mechanical operation.

Caproni, which had built the two prototypes, continued its interest, beginning the design of a high-altitude fighter to have been called the CA-183bis. It was to have used the 'thermojet' to boost the performance from a dreamed-of 460mph with just its 1,250hp Italian-built Daimler-Benz DB.605, to a purely imaginary 520mph with the assistance of a "thermojet" run by a 700hp A.30 radial engine.

To what extent the entire effort was motivated by the propaganda needs of Benito Mussolini's fascist government is not known, though the first announcements of the CC.2 certainly read that way.

Specifications

Length: 43ft 0in
Wingspan: 52ft 0in
Height: 15ft 5in
Wing area: 388 sq ft
Empty weight: 8,025lb
Maximum speed: 223mph
Maximum range: 310 miles
Service ceiling: 13,100ft

Surviving Example

487 – Italian Air Force Museum

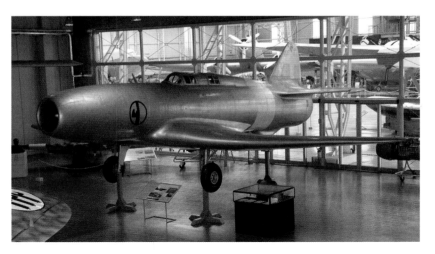

Chapter 9

Radio-Controlled

The concept of unmanned radio-controlled aircraft dates back at least to 1916, with Britain's Royal Flying Corps when an aerial target was being developed to attack German Zeppelins, which had been operating too high for current pursuits to intercept. In the U.S.A., the Hewitt-Sperry Automatic Airplane flew in September, 1916, demonstrating the eventual usefulness of the idea. In 1918, the Kettering "Bug", a flying bomb, flew too late to participate in World War I.

United States of America

ERCO XPQ-13 Ercoupe
A variety of standard and often obsolete military airplanes were equipped with radio controls, the result that some of the many problems were being solved. In the early 1930s, radio-controlled target airplanes were being developed in Britain and America, with the former being a modified Fairey IIIF being called the "Queen" which apparently led to future such devices being called "drones". The U.S. Navy experimented with a radio-controlled Curtiss N2C-2 Fledgling trainer that could be controlled from an airplane; these were in service as gunnery targets as early as 1938.

Among the standard airplanes considered by the U.S. Army Air Corps just prior to the U.S.A.'s entry into the war was the ERCO

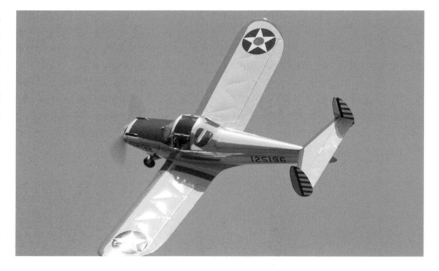

Ercoupe, an unspinable light plane with a simplified control system and an 85hp, four-cylinder Continental C-85 engine. Three were bought by the Army, one as a possible liaison plane, but which lost out to the classic Piper J-3 Cub (called the YO-55). The other two became XPQ-13s, but could not compete with the faster, more maneuverable Culver PQ-14, which also used less critical material in its structure.

Wing area: 143 sq ft
Empty weight: 750lb
Maximum speed: 110mph
Maximum range: 300 miles
Service ceiling: 13,000ft
Rate of climb: 550ft/min

Surviving Example

USAAC 41-25916 – Steven Hardin, Terrell, Texas

The Ercoupe went on to considerable post-war success in its original garb, with more than 5,000 being built by a long string of manufacturers. The Culver PQ-14 saw more than 800 built for the Army and almost 2,000 for the U.S. Navy as the TD2C.

Eventually, the relatively crude radio-control units and limited utility of the experimental phase gave way to today's ultra-high-tech UAVs that are replacing more and more manned combat aircraft.

Specifications

Length: 20ft 9in
Wingspan: 30ft 0in
Height: 5ft 11in

Culver PQ-14/TD2C-1

Al Mooney and his brother, Art (a famous band leader) started building small sport airplanes in 1939 with the Culver Dart and operating as the Culver Aircraft Co. In 1939, they began building the improved Model L or Culver Cadet. After building a few, they moved to Wichita, Kansas, answering a USAAF request for a simple low-wing airplane that could be used as a radio-controlled target drone and also flown cross-country by a pilot.

Their latest Cadet was modified, offered to the USAAF and accepted as the 125hp Lycoming-powered PQ-8, of which 400 were delivered, starting in 1942. It soon became the PQ-14 which was larger and faster, thanks to retractable landing gear. It was also built extensively from wood and thus pleased the AAF which was worried about the possible loss of aluminum as the Japanese captured more islands in the western Pacific.

Of the PQ-14A, 1,198 went to the U.S. Navy as the TD2C-1 and 150 to the USAAF. In 1944 almost 600 of the improved PQ-14B went to the Army, strictly for use as target drones, controlled mainly from twin-engined Beech C-45s. This rapidly reduced the supply, but as the tide of the war had turned, this did not seem to be a major problem.

The few PQ-14s that survived their "suicidal" missions were sold on the civilian market after the war, while the Culver Co. replaced them on the assembly line with the new and quite different Culver V. Its semi-automatic flight control system was not popular among pilots, many of whom had flown in the military, and so the type soon faded from the scene after fewer than 100 had been built.

An attempt to sell the USAAF a modified Culver V as the PQ-15 radio-controlled successor to the PQ-14 was not accepted. Culver then declared bankruptcy, the Mooney brothers forming a new company to build very popular airplanes under their own name. In the 1950s, the Culver V was bought by a new manufacturer who built it as the Superior Satellite.

Specifications

Length: 19ft 6in
Wingspan: 30ft 0in
Height: 8ft 5in
Wing area: 120 sq ft
Maximum weight: 1,830lb
Maximum speed: 185mph
Maximum range: 510 miles
Service ceiling: 17,000ft
Rate of climb: 910ft/min

Surviving Examples

PQ-14A
civil NL-15HM – Planes of Fame

PQ-14B
USAAF 44-21819 – Pima Air and Space Museum
USAAF 44-68334 – Experimental Aircraft Association
USAAF 44-68462 – National Museum of the U.S. Air Force
civil N5526A – Airpower Museum, Blakesburg, Iowa

TD2C-1
BuAer 120035 – U.S. National Air & Space Museum

Great Britain

deHavilland dH.82B "Queen Bee"
The deHavilland dH.82A Tiger Moth was a well established multi-purpose light plane when, in 1935, it was called upon to do its

Of 380 that were built, many by Scottish Aviation, Ltd., 375 went to the RAF for target work, and five to the Royal Navy, some of which had twin floats for use in live gunnery practice for ship-based guns.

Visually, they were almost indistinguishable from the far more common Tiger Moth trainers.

A follow-on target airplane – the Airspeed Queen Wasp – flew in 1940, one on wheels and one on floats. Sixty-five were ordered, but a total of just five were delivered due to shortcomings in power and water handling.

Specifications

Length: 23ft 11in
Wingspan: 29ft 4in
Height: 8ft 10in
Wing area: 239 sq ft
Empty weight: 1,115lb
Maximum speed: 109mph
Service ceiling: 13,600ft

Surviving Examples

RAF LF789 – deHavilland Heritage Museum
Flying with Capt. Neville's Flying Circus in England

military service as a radio-controlled drone providing an actual flying airplane at which coastal gunners could practice.

It was assembled from a dH.60-III Moth Major fuselage, Tiger Moth wings and tail, all built of wood, along with a 130hp Gypsy Major four-cylinder engine, a larger fuel tank and a wind-powered electrical generator. The prototype's first flight with a pilot on board was in January 1935.

Chapter 10

Miscellaneous

Some aircraft refuse to be categorized despite efforts to do so, unless "Miscellaneous" can be considered a category rather than an excuse. The airplanes under this heading were used for a variety of purposes, often quite different from what had originally been intended. Regardless, they deserve to be included in a volume such as this.

United States of America

Stinson V-77 "Gullwing"

It was a large airplane, sort of the aerial equivalent of a fine Packard motorcar of the late 1930s, with comfortable seats and plenty of head and foot room for those who appreciate the finer things in life. Power for most Reliants was the reliable 300hp, nine-cylinder Lycoming O-680 radial engine. While hundreds of them were built for the military during World War II, the designation "V-77" was a post-war appellation.

The first of a long series of gull-winged Reliants flew in 1933 as the SR-1, while the final SR-10 version flew in 1938 and was in production until 1941. The U.S. military's first was the AT-19, a modified and somewhat simplified version of the SR-10, 500 of which were ordered in 1942 as navigational trainers from Vultee, which had recently merged with Stinson. Sometime between

ordering and delivery, it was decided they were not needed and were sent to Great Britain as part of the huge Lend-Lease program involving almost every type of military equipment. The Reliant Mk.1 was used as a small transport for specialized missions, the Mk.2 had increased radio equipment for training navigators, and the Mk.3 was used to train observers and aerial photographers, and the Mk.4 carried small cargo shipments.

Detecting a new need for airplanes of the Reliant class, the U.S. Army Air Forces impressed several dozen civilian Gullwings of various versions, designating them UC-81A through -81N.

After the war, more than 350 of the 500 sent to Britain were returned to the U.S.A., were given the "V-77" designation and sold on the war surplus market for as little as $1,500, depending on their condition. Many are still flying as prized classic airplanes and can be seen at vintage fly-ins.

Specifications

Length: 29ft 6in
Wingspan: 41ft 10in
Height: 9ft 2in
Empty weight: 2,530lb
Cruising Speed: 152mph
Maximum range: 650 miles
Service ceiling: 12,700ft

Surviving Examples

Many with private owners

Great Britain

Avro 504K

It was used as a fighter and a bomber, and then for reconnaissance and training. And that was just in World War *One*. Later it was the standard trainer for the RAF well into the 1930s, and was resurrected in 1940 as a target and glider tug. With more than 10,000 built, it was a dominant feature of the military and civilian flying scenes.

The first flight of the 80hp Gnome rotary engine-powered prototype was in September 1913, more than a year before the start

of "The War To End All Wars". Four 504s of the Royal Naval Air Service (RNAS) did major damage to a German Zeppelin factory, though each carried but four 20lb hand-held bombs. Later in the war, several 504Ks were equipped with a single .30 cal. machine gun and more powerful rotary engines, to be used for home defense by the Royal Flying Corps (RFC).

For most of the war, the 504K was the standard military and naval trainer, with hundreds of those that had survived being sold as surplus and used for training private pilots, joy-riding for those who had fallen under the spell of the overly glamorized tales of aerial dogfights, and for towing commercial advertising banners. This continued into the 1930s, when more modern airplanes such as the deHavilland Gypsy Moth and then Tiger Moth made flying safer and more economical.

Starting in 1925, the 504 was modernized with the installation of successive models of the Armstrong-Siddeley Lynx V radial engine, producing from 180 to 215hp and giving accompanying increases in performance. Almost 600 were manufactured from 1925 to 1932 and were used at every RAF flying school, as well as in other countries in Europe, Africa, Asia, South America and North America.

It was in 1933 that the venerable Avro 504 was finally replaced as the standard RAF trainer by Avro's Tutor. The 504 wasn't completely forgotten, as seven were impressed from their civilian owners and used as tow planes, remaining in service as late as 1940.

Specifications

Length: 29ft 5in
Wingspan: 35ft 0in
Height: 10ft 5in
Wing area: 330 sq ft
Empty weight: 1,230lb
Maximum speed: 90mph
Maximum range: 250 miles
Service ceiling: 16,000ft
Rate of climb: 700ft/min

Surviving Examples

Shuttleworth Collection, Old Warden Aerodrome
Science Museum, London

Westland Wallace

The first Westland Wapiti general purpose biplane was built from parts of a World War II-era deHavilland dH.9, and the first Wallace

replacement was built from a Wapiti. In the between-the-wars period, cautious steps were preferred in those days of limited funds for military aircraft.

The Wapiti Mk.I first flew with a 420hp Bristol Jupiter in 1927 and soon was ordered for service in Iraq. It was followed by the Mk.II which had an up-rated engine and served mainly in the UK. The final version was the Mk.VI, a limited production dual-control trainer. Wapitis performed a variety of roles, including Army co-operation and communication, as well as light bombing and reconnaissance. Most were retired by 1937, though a few were still in RAF service in India as late as 1939.

The first Wallace was a converted Wapiti, built in 1931 with a longer fuselage, faired, fixed landing gear and a 650hp Bristol Pegasus IV engine. It, and the Westland PV-3 prototype torpedo bomber, became the first airplanes to fly over Mount Everest in 1933.

The first group of 68 Wallace Mk.I was composed of modified Wapitis, with the major Mk.II version having a full cockpit cover and a 680hp Pegasus radial engine. Most of the 104 were assigned to the Auxiliary Air Force, which used them as general purpose airplanes, and then as target tugs.

Manufacturing was completed in 1936, but the operation of these clearly obsolete airplanes continued. When the war began, more than 80 were still in use, not being retired completely until 1943.

Specifications

Length: 34ft 2in
Wingspan: 46ft 5in
Height: 11ft 6in
Wing area: 488 sq ft
Empty weight: 3,840lb
Maximum speed: 158mph
Maximum range: 470 miles
Service ceiling: 24,100ft
Rate of climb: 1,350ft/min

Surviving Example

RAF 6035 – RAF Museum Hendon,

France

Mignet HM-280 Pou-du-Ciel

Has there ever been an aircraft displaying less military adaptability than the cute little Flying Flea? After all, its designer, Henri Mignet,

created it because he had decided he could not learn to fly an airplane. It had a simplified control system that was supposed to make it stall- and spin-proof, and a payload equal to its builder's weight. If ever there was a flying machine that qualified for the "puddle-jumper" description, it was le Pou.

Mignet flew his first Pou, the HM.14, in 1933 and soon published drawings and detailed building instructions which were eagerly grabbed up by fascinated Frenchmen: carpenters and mechanics, as well as cooks and waiters, none of whom had any experience building aircraft, and few of whom had received any flying instruction. The mania spread around Europe and to far-flung areas such as the U.S.A., where thousands of Pou building projects were launched with far more enthusiasm than knowledge.

Soon, one and then several more Poux were involved in fatal accidents, eventually blamed on a design flaw which turned a mild descent into an increasingly steep dive, from which recovery was extremely difficult, especially at low altitude. This led, predictably, to the Pou being outlawed in one and then in many countries. The correction of the design flaw came too late to save the Pou and the budding amateur-construction movement which it had triggered.

After the fall of France in 1940, resistance groups were formed, gradually merging into larger units as the suffering increased and the need to fight back by blowing up bridges and trucks increased. Eventually, quasi-military organizations emerged, becoming a major problem to the occupying Nazis as they began to go on the offensive. The need for a light airplane that could operate off dirt roads and be easy to transport and hide came to the attention of Maquis Gen. Eon.

The result was an order for several HM.280 "Pou-Maquis" with folding wings, and the delivery of at least four was achieved. They were used to transport people (one at a time), as well as critical materiel. One is rumored to have been used by two men to escape across the English Channel.

Typical Specifications

Length: 14ft 0in
Wingspan: 20ft 0in
Wing area: 94 sq ft
Empty weight: 400lb
Maximum speed: 85mph

Maximum range: 275 miles
Service ceiling: 16,400ft
Rate of climb: 600ft/min

Surviving Example

An actual Pou-Maquis may be in the Musee des Arts et Metiers, Paris
The HM.280 formerly in the RAF Millom Museum, was a reproduction

Germany

Messerschmitt Bf.108 Typhoon
The Treaty of Versailles did not prohibit the building of sporting aircraft in post-World War I Germany. A variety of gliders, sailplanes and light airplanes filled the need for a few sporting pilots and a lot more future fighter and bomber pilots who needed low-performance aircraft for their primary training. Among the dual-purpose machines was the Bf-108, the prototype of which made its initial flight in 1934.

At least seven Bf-108As were built expressly for the 4th International Touring Planes Challenge, a bi-annual event encompassing a variety of tests of airplanes and pilots, held in Warsaw, Poland. While the Poles repeated their 1932 over-all victory, followed by the Germans in their Messerschmitts, the Germans swept the 297km. closed course speed competition.

This was followed by a series of long-distance class records, thanks to the Bf-108's combination of speed, low fuel consumption and generally good handling characteristics.

Specifications

Length: 27ft 2in
Wingspan: 34ft 5in
Height: 7ft 6in
Wing area: 172 sq ft
Empty weight: 1,775lb
Maximum speed: 190mph
Maximum range: 620 miles
Service ceiling: 20,300ft
Rate of climb: 1,200ft/min

Surviving Example

Bf-108B-2
c/n 2083 – Museum der Schweizerischen, Fliegertruppe, Dubendorf,
   Germany
The Fighter Factory

Nord 1202
c/n183 – Imperial War Museum, Duxford

The Bf-108A used a 250hp Hirth HM 8U inverted V-12 engine, while the 108B had a 240hp Argus As 10 inverted V-8, though the prototype had a 170hp Siemens Sh 14A seven-cylinder radial engine. The 108C was to have been a high-speed model with a 395hp Hirth HM 512 inverted V-12. Most of the 800-plus airplanes which the French built under duress for the Germans were used as liaison and personnel transports.

A major development was the Me-208 ("Bf" for the Bavarian Aircraft Works, was changed to honor chief designer Messerschmitt with "Me"). It was larger and had the increasingly popular tricycle landing gear. The war ended soon after two prototypes were built in the Nord factory in occupied France, after which it remained in production as the Nord Noralpha. Other Bf-108 successors were the slightly modified Nord 101 and the Renault-powered Nord 1002.

Siebel Si.204D

It was to have been a short-haul airliner for Lufthansa, and a few were actually delivered as such. But when the war began, production was taken over by the Luftwaffe, and all further airplanes are marked by windshields which are flush with the nose contours.

Plans for the eight-passenger airliner were put into motion in 1938, though the prototype didn't fly until mid-1940. Due to

Specifications

Length: 42ft 8in
Wingspan: 70ft 0in
Height: 14ft 0in
Wing area: 495 sq ft
Empty weight: 8,700lb
Maximum speed: 228mph
Maximum range: 875 miles
Service ceiling: 21,000 ft
Rate of climb: 1,200ft/min

Surviving Examples

Aero C 3A
c/n 350 – (modified from NC.702) Aircraft Service & Restoration, Prague, Czech Republic
civil OK-ADZ – Slovenske Dopravni Muzeum, Presov

NC.702
c/n 282 – Musee de l'Air, on loan to Conservatoire de l'Aeronautique at de l'Space d'Aquitane,
Merignaz AB, Bordeaux
c/n 331 – Deutches Technik Museum, Berlin

Siebel's preoccupation with Ju.88 bomber manufacture, only a few Si.204s were built by the designer, with all 115 model Si.204A being built by SNCAN in occupied France. The model "D" blind-flying trainers were constructed by BMM and Aero, both in occupied Czechoslovakia, aside from some 50 by SNCAN.

The Si-204A series were used for communications duties and to provide more comfortable transportation for senior officers. 204Ds were used mainly as advanced trainers and for ferrying Luftwaffe delivery pilots back to their home bases. When the situation was becoming desperate, five 204s were somehow modified into night fighters, though they apparently never got as far as combat action.

After the war, captured Siebels were used briefly by the U.S.S.R. as feeder airliners and for some experimental work

Extinct Other Types Of World War II Aircraft

Transports

U.S.A.
Stout C-65 Skycar
Spartan C-71 Executive
Waco C-72
Boeing C-73/civil 237
Curtiss C-76 Caravan
Harlow C-80PJC
Piper C-83
Lockheed C-85 Orion
Fairchild C-88F-45
Hamilton C-89H-47
Luscombe C-908
Stinson C-91SM-6000
Akron-Funk C-92B-75-L
Cessna C-94 Airmaster
Fairchild C-96F-71
Boeing C-98/civil 314 Clipper
Northrop C-1002-D Gamma
Lockheed C-1015-C Vega
Rearwin C-102/civil 9000KR
Boeing C-105 (XB-115) transport
Stout C-107 Skycar IIIA

Douglas C-110 DC-5
Lockheed C-111
Curtiss C-113
Douglas C-117

Great Britain
deHavilland 86
deHavilland 95 Flamingo
Handley-Page Harrow
Armstrong Whitworth Albemarle
Miles M-57 Aerovan

France
Bloch MB.81
Bloch MB.220
Caudron C.630
Potez 402
Potez 662
SE.200

Germany
Junkers Ju.89
Junkers Ju.90
Junkers Ju.390

Heinkel He.116
Focke Wulf FW.200 Condor
Blohm & Voss BV.144
Blohm & Voss BV.222 Viking
Messerschmitt Me.323Gigant
Arado Ar.232
Gotha Go.244

Japan
Tachikawa Ki.54
Kawasaki Ki.56
Mitsubishi Ki.57 "Topsy"
Nakajima G5N1 "Liz"
Nakajima Ki.34 "Thora"

Trainers

U.S.A.
Waco PT-14UPF-7
St. Louis PT-15
deHavilland DHC PT-24 Tiger Moth
Fleetwings BT-12
Boeing BT-17
Fairchild AT-13
Boeing AT-15
Lockheed AT-18
Vultee AT-19
Federal AT-20 Anson
Fairchild AT-21

Great Britain
Miles M.18
Hawker Nimrod
Airspeed A.S.45
Bristol Buckmaster

Germany
Arado Ar.96
Henschel Hs.125
Ha.136
Bucker Bu.180 Student
Bucker Bu.186 Kornett

Japan
Mitsubishi K3M
Kyushu K11W Shiragiku

Reconnaissance

U.S.A.
Curtiss SO3C Seagull/Seamew
Curtiss SC Seahawk
Hughes F-11

Great Britain
Vickers Vildebeest
Saro London
Short Singapore
Short S-35 Shetland
Short Seaford

Scapa
Saro Lerwick
Vickers-Armstrong Warwick
Airspeed AS.39 Fleet Shadower
General Aircraft GAL 38
Blackburn Shark
Fairey Seafox
Blackburn B.20

France

Mureaux 110
Bloch M.B.174
Breguet 270
Dewoitine D.720
Hanriot NC.530

Union of Soviet Socialist Republics

MBR-2

Germany

Heinkel He.114
Blohm & Voss BV.144
Gotha Go.145
Messerschmitt Me.323 Gigant
Dornier Do.18 Whale
Henschel He.126

Japan

Aichi E16A1 "Paul"
Kawanishi H6K5 "Mavis"
Kawanishi E15K1 "Norm"
Tokosuku E14Y1 "Glen"

Rotary Wing

Germany

Focke Achgelis FA.223

Liaison

Germany

Henschel Hs.126
Gotha Go.150

Gliders

U.S.A.

Piper TG-8
Laister-Kauffman CG-10A
Waco CG-13
Waco CG-15

Great Britain

General Aircraft Hotspur
General Aircraft Twin Hotspur

Germany

DFS.228
Kalkart Ka.430
Messerschmitt Me.321

Research

Great Britain
Folland 33/37
Miles M.28
Miles M.35
Miles M.39B

Germany
Heinkel He.176
Heinkel He.178
Henschel Hs.128

Miscellaneous

Great Britain
Miles Falcon
Miles M.25 Martinet
Miles M.33 Monitor
Fairey Seal
Miles M.11a Whitney Straight
Percival Q6

Germany
Arado Ar.95
Henschel Hs.124
Gotha Go.

Appendix B

Museums With Large Collections Of World War II Aircraft

North America

National Air & Space Museum, Washington, D.C. Main building on The Mall in the center of the city. Newer Udvar-Hazy Center annex near Dulles International Airport, 30 miles to the west, in Virginia. Closed December 25. Hours: 10:00 a.m. to 5:30 p.m.; summer (May 22 to September 7) Mall Bldg. open 10:00 a.m. to 7:30 p.m., Udvar-Hazy 10:00 a.m. to 8:30 p.m. No charge for admission, but $15 for car parking at Udvar-Hazy. www.nasm.si.edu

The National Museum of the U.S. Air Force (formerly called the U.S. Air Force Museum), north of Dayton, Ohio, on the Wright-Patterson Air Force Base. Closed Thanksgiving (4th Thursday in November), Christmas and New Year's Day. Hours: 9:00 a.m. to 5:00 p.m. No charge for admission or parking. www.AFmuseum.com

The National Museum of Naval Aviation, Pensacola Naval Air Station, Pensacola, Florida. Closed New Year's Day, Thanksgiving and Christmas. Hours: 9:00 a.m. to 5:00 p.m. No charge for admission or parking. www.navalaviationmuseum.org

Planes of Fame, 7000 Merrill Ave., Chino Airport, Chino, California. Open from 9:00 a.m. to 5:00 p.m. every day except Thanksgiving and Christmas. **Planes of Fame – Grand Canyon** annex museum is at the Grand Canyon-Valle Airport, Valle, Arizona. General admission $11.00; children between 5 and 11 $4.00. www.planesoffame.org

Experimental Aircraft Association AirVenture Museum, Wittman Regional Airport, Oshkosh, Wisconsin. Open from 8:30 a.m. to 5:00 p.m. except Sunday opening at 10:00 a.m. Open every day except New Year's Day, Easter Sunday, Thanksgiving and Christmas. Admission: $12.50 except seniors 62 and older $10.50, students aged 6–17 $9.50, under 6 and EAA members free. www.airventuremuseum.org

Pima Air and Space Museum, 6000 E. Valencia Rd., Tucson, Arizona, adjacent to Davis-Monthan AFB. Open daily from 9:00 a.m. to 5:00 p.m, except Thanksgiving and Christmas. Admission (June–October) $13.75 for adults 13 and older, for seniors and military $11.75, for students 7–12 $8.00. (November–May) $15.50 for adults, $12.75 for seniors and military, $9.00 for students. Five and under free. www.pimaair.org

New England Air Museum, Bradley International Airport, Windsor Locks, Connecticut. Open daily (except Thanksgiving, Christmas and New Years Day) from 10 a.m. to 5 p.m. Admission:

adults 12 and older $10, seniors 65 and older $9, children 4–11 $6, 3 and under free. www.neam.org

Fantasy of Flight, 1400 Broadway Blvd., Polk City, Florida. Open 9 a.m. to 5 p.m. every day except Thanksgiving and Christmas. Admission: adults $28.95, Youths 6–15 $14.95, 5 and under free. www.fantasyofflight.com

Canadian Aviation Museum, 11 Aviation Parkway, Ottawa, Ontario. Open every day but Christmas, and Monday–Tuesday from September through April. May through August, 9 a.m. to 5 p.m.; September through April, 10 a.m. to 5 p.m. Admission: adults $9, students and seniors $6, ages 4–15, $5; under 4 and veterans free. www.aviationtechnomuses.ca

Great Britain

Royal Air Force Museum, **Hendon**, Grahame Park Way, Colindale, North London. Most halls open from 10 a.m. to 6 p.m. every day except from Christmas eve through the 26th, New Year's Day and January 10–15. No charge for admission. Colindale Underground station. www.rafmuseum.com

Royal Air Force Museum, Cosford, Shifnal, Shropshire. Most exhibits open every day except Christmas Eve, Christmas Day and Boxing Day (December 26), and New Year's Day, from 10 a.m. to 6 p.m. No charge for admission. www.rafmuseumcosford.org.uk.

Imperial War Museum, RAF Duxford, Cambridgeshire (at Junction 10 of M11 motorway). Open every day but December 24–26, between late October and mid-March from 10 a.m. to 4 p.m., otherwise 10 a.m. to 6 p.m. Admission: ages 0 to 15 Free; 16–59 £16.00; 60+ and students £12.80, disabled £9.60. www.duxford.iwm,org.uk

Fleet Air Arm Museum, Royal Naval Air Station Yeovilton, Somerset. Open every day except December 24–26, from early April to late October 10 a.m. to 5:30 p.m., and other times from 10 a.m. to 4:30 p.m. except closed Mondays and Tuesdays. Admission: adults ages 17+ £11.00; youth 5–16 £8.00; seniors, students and veterans £9.00. www.fleetairarm.com

Midland Air Museum, Coventry Airport, Baginton, Warwickshire. Open every day but December 25–26. April through October 10 a.m. to 5 p.m., November through March 10:30 a.m. to 4:30 p.m. Admission: adults 17+ £5.25, youth 5–16 £2.75, under age 5 Free, retirees and students £4.75. www.midlandairmuseum.com

Shuttleworth Collection, Old Warden Aerodrome, Old Warden, Bedfordshire. Open every day except Christmas week and New Year's Day. Winter open 10 a.m. to 4 p.m.; Summer open 10 a.m. to 5 p.m. Admission: adults £10, seniors £9, children up to 16 years Free. www.shuttleworth.org

France

Musee de l'Air et de l'Espace (Air and Space Museum), le Bourget Aeroport, a few miles north of Paris. No charge for admission. Open every day but Monday; April through September, 10 a.m. to 6 p.m.; October through March, 10 a.m. to 5 p.m. www.mae.org

Belgium

Brussels Air Museum, Parc du Cinquantenaire, Brussels. Open 9 a.m. to 4:30 p.m. every day but Monday; closed on official public holidays. Admission free. www.airmuseum.be

Italy

Museo Storico dell'Aeronautica Militaire (Italian Air Force Museum), Vigna di Valle, northwest of Rome, along the west shore of Lake Garda. Open June–September from 9:30 a.m. to 5:30 p.m., and otherwise from 9:30 a.m. to 4:30 p.m., except closed on New Year's Day, Easter Sunday, Christmas and every Monday. Admission free. www.aeronautica.difesa,it

Poland

Muzeum Lotnictwa Polskiego (Polish Air Museum), a few miles east of Kracow. Open every day: Monday (for outdoor exhibits only) 9 a.m. to 3:30 p.m., free. Tuesday–Friday 9 a.m. to 5 p.m., Saturday and Sunday 10 a.m. to 4 p.m. Admission: adults 5 zlotys, children 3 zlotys, www.muzeumlotnictwa.pl